A Humanitarian's Defense of Capitalism

A Humanitarian's Defense of Capitalism

The Paradigm of Freedom

2016

Paul R. Martel

ISBN: 1523462906
ISBN 13: 9781523462902
Library of Congress Control Number: 2016902106
CreateSpace Independent Publishing Platform
North Charleston, South Carolina

This book is dedicated to my dear grandchildren and to the next generation of Americans. May they always know the same opportunity and freedom with which I have been blessed.

Foreword

I began writing about the two worlds I live and work in during the winter of 2016, a time of great and increasingly unsettled change. Fear and widening opinions about our future path as a nation are consuming an overwhelming number of Americans including myself. Countless polls reveal that 48% of young adults in the U.S. today feel that the American dream is dying. A great many Americans are frustrated and angry; and rightly so. In fact, a CNN/ORC poll conducted in December 2015 suggests that 69% of Americans are either "very angry" or "somewhat angry" about the way things are progressing in the US.

William Galston, an expert in governance at the Brookings Institution is quoted in a BBC article with a poignant explanation: *"The failure of the economy to deliver real progress to middle-class and working class Americans over the last 15 years is the most fundamental source of public anger and disaffection in the US."*

While our country has recovered from the recent recession, our economy remains weak, many are without jobs or underemployed and incomes are shrinking. The cost of housing, health care and education is making it nearly impossible for many families to make ends meet. Our immigration system is broken and globalization seems like a curse to many American workers. Our national debt is now approaching $19 trillion and our debt "limit" is a work of fiction. Unthinkable only decades ago, a growing percentage of Americans concludes that socialism is a preferable economic system. It is no coincidence that, as I write this, a socialist candidate is drawing large, enthusiastic crowds in his run for the Presidency. Bernie Sanders has provided a perfect excuse for those Americans looking for answers and someone or something to blame. Capitalism is under attack and on trial. The reason for this book is to say as clearly and forcefully as I can, "You've got the wrong guy." I despair deeply at this trend and view it as a danger signal and a significant threat to our nation's well-being. Capitalism has generated life altering prosperity, innovation, advancement, modernisms and hope throughout the world. Its success is evident from the simplicity of electricity and transportation to the internet, computers and the medical miracles of vaccines and organ transplants. The socialist view is that all the good induced by Capitalism is iniquitous and unethical. Essentially, that those who have more are bad for society and that economic inequality is unfair and intolerable.

It is this fundamental thought that inspires me to write this book because I am a man who lives two lives in two very different worlds. In one, I am a capitalist and long-time business owner. In the other, I am a humanitarian. My experience as founder of a successful investment management firm gives me an informed and thoughtful point of view of our domestic and global economies and investment markets. The success I have had, in turn, makes it possible for me to use my prosperity to fund humanitarian endeavors, perhaps not on the same scale as Bill Gates, but sharing the same principal; we are capitalists who believe that our materialistic acquisitions are worthless unless our capital serves humanity and a greater good. My success allows me to bring necessary medical care to children and families desperate for even the simplest assistance in South America.

I live in two separate and very contrasting worlds; to some, incompatible, but together profoundly powerful and meaningful. Living in both these worlds provides a striking contradiction because the economic systems in the foreign countries in which I work are dramatically different from what we know and live here in the United States.

In my humanitarian life, I operate in countries that are drenched in socialism. I have traveled and worked extensively in Ecuador, Colombia, Paraguay and Guatemala, countries with strong socialist traditions. The reality of my involvement and experience influenced me tremendously and motivated me to establish a foundation and a surgical center in Riobamba, Ecuador. Through these efforts, I have learned to work and survive in broken countries with extreme poverty and perpetual political, social and economic problems.

The people we serve have little or nothing at all including almost no access to health care. They live in communities awash in crime and depraved violence. They nod as their leaders decry the U.S. and its capitalist system but have absolutely no knowledge of how it differs from their own. Their suffering is real and their economies inescapably crippled. Socialism is not theoretical to me or to the people who live in these countries. We face its failure and the consequences of that failure every day. It is this perspective I want to share.

I make no pretense that this is a scholarly work, only that I believe it is exceedingly relevant. Our country faces very significant economic challenges and in my effort to identify them I will remind readers that our problems do not lie in our freedoms or the free enterprise system from which we all derive our livings and prosperity. I am not naïve to the excesses of capitalism, to the frustrations of struggling Americans or to the significant damage that was done in the recent mortgage and banking crisis. Indeed, the recent receptiveness among progressives to socialist ideas may come largely from that crisis. I would argue, though, that such events were not caused by flaws in our system but weaknesses in our natures as human beings. It was not our economic system that caused the mortgage crisis, but the irresponsibility and greed of lenders, bank executives, and mortgage salesmen and the consequences of well-intentioned but unwise political policies. Further, destructive and immoral business practices were leveraged by the steroid effect of powerful technology that few can understand or control. We must be clear as a people where the true blame lies lest we cut off our noses to spite our faces. Pete Rose's gambling on baseball was not caused by the sport itself. Bernie Madoff was nothing but a sophisticated crook. His crimes were caused by him and not by capitalism. Those who conclude otherwise are throwing the baby out with the bathwater, and are committing an egregious error. Socialism is gaining a foothold in the United States and our paradigm is changing in subtle ways that you may not yet be noticing but might someday regret.

We are at great risk of jeopardizing our legacy by not teaching the basics of our unparalleled economic system and the great potential it offers to those willing to participate. Capitalism is a powerful but widely misunderstood tool. Better that we should teach its use in a responsible and moral way than to tear it down. We do that at our extreme peril.

This book is born in part from now commonplace public statements from progressive politicians that all run like the following:

> *There is nobody in this country who got rich on his own, nobody. You built a factory out there, good for you. But I want to be clear. You moved your goods to market on the roads the rest of us paid for. You hired workers the rest of us paid to educate. You built a factory, and it turned into something terrific or a great idea—God bless! Keep a big hunk of it. But part of the underlying*

*social contract is you take a hunk of that and
pay forward for the next kid who comes along.*

The messages in this short paragraph are poison; so much the worse that they come from senior U.S. officials. The words imply gross falsehoods in a way we should all find repulsive: That the business owner has taken something from others ("the rest of us"); that he or she used other people's money; that the owner has not also paid taxes to build roads and educate workers; that the owner's business has not also paid taxes; that business owners are, in effect, thieves; that government has the right to decide what "hunk" the owner is entitled to; that the owner owes an extra "hunk" because of the way he or she supposedly abused our system. This is the ugly theme song of the New Left. There are many variations of it and people are humming the tunes. It would be hard for me to imagine public positions that could be more irresponsible, slanderous and insulting to our heritage as a free people or to our population of business owners. Just to be clear, business owners don't take anything from anyone to start their businesses, they most often take out loans; a risk they themselves bear. They are not, then, using other people's money but risking their own. They pay taxes for roads and schools just like everyone else. There is no "rest of us!" Their businesses also pay taxes for the same services. Lastly, the government has no moral or constitutional right to say what the owner is or is not entitled to. And I have one question: By taking risk and creating jobs, commerce and wealth, exactly what part of this imaginary social contract are they breaking?

Nevertheless, as we speak, these words are echoing in many other high level speeches and spawning other handy words and phrases to quickly convey the same sorry, deceptive message. The business owner is clearly the new enemy in a new chapter of class warfare. It is nothing short of a pathetic state of affairs.

Shuttling back and forth between two political and economic worlds as I do highlights their differences and, brings them into dramatic focus. By sharing some observations, perhaps I can serve as a "canary in the coal mine" and raise awareness that we are farther down a harmful path than you might have thought.

None of this is to suggest that each of us should be entrepreneurs or pursue a life in business. Our country and our lives are richer for the gifts of artists, writers, designers, police, firemen, and teachers. What it does suggest, though, is an urgent need for a new national consensus; an accord that recognizes and respects the vital importance of the enterprise, commerce and prosperity that make our communities and our nation strong. Ripping apart the foundation of our economic system will help no one and make our problems infinitely worse.

Among the chapters that follow, I have inserted stories of the humanitarian work that I and countless other Americans do. They serve to illustrate, in a real way, not only the downside of the socialist paradigm but the power that our prosperity holds for those who wish to affect change in the world.

Paul R. Martel

The absence of freedom and prosperity creates a life strikingly different from the one we know. These stories seek to show the reality of life in societies without opportunity, capital, hope or access to public services such as health care. I will share personal observations to explore the subtle but profound differences between Capitalism and Socialism. These observations will illustrate powerful but fragile traditions of thinking that most Americans now take for granted and may lose. Part of this book's message is a call to educators at all levels to begin teaching students about our country's economic traditions.

Rather than dwelling on the flaws of our system, which certainly exist, they should teach our young people how to use our unique and powerful engine for their own benefit and for the benefit of others. We should encourage this not just for what it can mean for their futures but what it can mean for our communities and the wider world. By dwelling on the weaknesses of our system and not its potential, too many students graduate with an antagonism that poisons and distorts the function and role of our economy and how they can fit in. The person who said that you don't know what you've got till its gone, could never have imagined what we are putting at risk by not appreciating, teaching and supporting the unique way we Americans have organized ourselves economically. It is called capitalism and it functions in what I call The Paradigm of Freedom.

THE PARADIGM OF FREEDOM

In my humanitarian work, I travel to Central and South American countries roughly five times a year. I have just returned from a relief effort in Ecuador which was rocked by a devastating earthquake that left more than 650 people dead and countless lives, cities and communities shattered. These were my thoughts: After traveling for 34 hours, I finally arrive in Pedernales, the heart of the destruction caused by the magnitude 7.8 earthquake. As I look around at the sheer devastation, I am visibly moved by the horror that lay before me. In just 3 minutes, a tremor from inside the earth's surface has forced tens of thousands into crude shelters disbursed along the highways, separated from the families, friends and lives they once knew. The group I am traveling with immediately visits two of these roadside refuges to distribute water, diapers and clothes. The people are drawn to our headlights like ghosts coming out of the night carrying their children and babies. I have no idea what they are hoping for or exactly how their circumstances would improve. The measure of ruin and the depth of the poverty are paralyzing. The stench of death hangs in the air with an unforgiving cruelty as the earth continues to shake beneath them.

We drive for two hours through the streets of the crumbled city of Pedernales with our mouths agape under our masks. Our objective, representing my foundation, Fibuspam, is to find the command center located in the local stadium to meet with the military commanders to get approval for a medical caravan to the area. The stadium is packed with scores of police, military, firemen, aid groups such as the Red Cross and volunteers. I am immediately struck by the tent marked "desaparecidos" for those people still seeking loved ones who remain missing. I imagine the hundreds who are still unfound in the massive rubble. We meet with two leaders who welcome our proposal and suggest several remote communities that are not yet receiving aid. They are actually glad that we were planning our caravan a few weeks out on May 8th due to commitments to two foreign groups at the clinic. They say that the international urgency and attention would subside soon and the people will become more forgotten.

As we walk back to the car, I notice the large number of 4-5 story hotels. This region is a very popular tourist area and the hotels were busy that night with guests, many now buried forever in the piles of debris. Looking at some of these buildings, one is easily deceived to believe the damage is not so extensive until you realize that at ground level you are looking at the second floor. The first floors have simply vanished.

There are many migrants from the Andes and Chimborazo province in this area. They come here seeking the financial opportunity that tourism provides. Many of these people have lost everything they gained over the last 10-15 years and will limp back to their communities in the Andes. One family was not so fortunate. They are from the town of Ukshapamba in the canton of Colta. They fled to Pedernales about 10 years ago and established their own hotel. The entire family was killed when the hotel collapsed. The sadness is even more crushing when you realize that, even in the face of humanitarian disaster and relief, racism is inescapable for the indigenous who immigrated to this area. I am told that they are often passed over when water and other provisions are distributed by local authorities.

As we continue our long journey, I see that death's hand has reached all the way to Riobamba, the home of my foundation, Fibuspam, 7 hours away. A woman was dining in a local restaurant when the quake struck. Becoming afraid the building might collapse, she ran out of the restaurant into the street where she was struck and killed by a piece of falling cement. In another local incident, because it had rained for six hours before the quake struck, a large pool of water had formed above a small neighborhood. When the shaking started, the water started a landslide that washed away three houses and killed three children.

Life is painfully hard for the people of Ecuador and for hundreds of thousands in six provinces, it just got much harder. Indeed, the disaster will cost all 16 million Ecuadorians dearly.

In an already struggling economy, four new taxes have been levied to help pay for the recovery efforts. The cost of rebuilding is estimated in the billions.

What interrupts the heartache and hopelessness is seeing help arrive not just from all parts of the country but from so many foreign countries. I am so proud that our organization can lend a hand and provide medical care and comfort to those whose suffering is still so raw. I am especially grateful to our supporters in the U.S. who are helping to make this care possible.

At the conclusion of all my trips, I return to the U.S. and marvel with pride at what we have built together as a nation. I admire the stability and quality of our institutions, the freedom we have to choose our own paths in life, and the opportunity we all have to succeed. I am proud of our enduring systems of law and governance and the respect we have for them, the wealth and talent we share with other nations, and the powerful and efficient systems of banking, capital and investment markets that fuel our individual and collective prosperity.

Returning home from countries that have none of these benefits and privileges, one cannot help but feel profoundly blessed. And yet, upon returning, I am faced with a surprising lack of understanding and appreciation, indeed a growing, outright antagonism for the economic system that makes our country so unique and strong. I journey back to the U.S. from environments of hopelessness, gross poverty and suffering to find apathy and an absence of any comprehension of our own economic system and freedoms. This is always a shock to me. My confusion and disappointment is profound and for years I have tried to understand how this can be conceivable and what it may hold for our future. How can it be that millions of people long for the economic system, freedom and opportunity that so many of our own citizens have so little understanding of or gratitude for? How can we as a people be so apathetic and disapproving of a system that so many risk their lives to attain?

People organize themselves personally and collectively around shared ideas. These ideas shape our thinking and provide the framework on which we build our lives, our families and our communities. We call these ideas paradigms. An illustration of this is in the words of Bob Dylan, *"Those that aren't busy being born are busy dying."* Here we see two distinct paradigms, two ways to approach life, work and relationships. While the individual daily manifestations of each approach might seem subtle, the outcomes are dramatically different. Nothing could be more important than the fundamental idea around which you shape your life.

For 250 years, Americans have built their individual and collective lives around the paradigm of freedom. It is the most fundamental feature of who we are as Americans. It is codified in our Constitution and our Bill of Rights. It shapes our laws, our form of governance, our thoughts and self-images, our workplaces, worship, speech, education and the way we form our families. It also shapes our shared economic lives. Remove the paradigm of freedom and our society would descend into chaos. There is nothing more fundamental to us as a people. We collectively believe there is a moral imperative to freedom; that the natural state of a human being is to live in freedom and that by being free, we live lives with more dignity, purpose and meaning. We hold these truths to be self-evident, do we not? Richard John Neuhaus believed so:

> *"The (American) experiment will continue so long as the truths are held. When Americans can no longer persuasively articulate the truths of freedom, they will discover to their dismay that there are many ways to order society other than freedom."*

We live in a Paradigm of Freedom and we are fortunate for it; but I fear our indifference.

The Paradigm of Freedom also shapes our individual and collective economic lives. In every way imaginable, our capitalist system springs directly from it. Capitalism is the economic expression of our personal freedom. Indeed, it cannot exist without it.

Back in 2007, I opened a small, free health clinic in Riobamba, Ecuador, a country with close ties to Cuba,

Venezuela and other leftist, socialist countries. On my second visit to the clinic, I was delighted to find a small, framed photo of myself on the wall of our simple waiting area. I was incredibly touched by this gesture but my emotions quickly morphed into melancholy and discouragement as I noticed something that spoke volumes about this place that was becoming like a second home. Next to my small photo was a very large portrait of Che Guevara, a famous Cuban, socialist revolutionary and partner of Fidel Castro. Che was killed waging a similar battle in Bolivia. He is a revered, heroic figure throughout South America and an icon in leftist circles. It is not unusual to see entire walls with Che's image in the offices of public officials in Ecuador. His image on the wall can invoke feelings of vulnerability and cause meetings to contain a cloud of fear. As I looked back and forth at the two pictures, it was clear where I stood in the pecking order and that I had much to learn about the nature of economic life in Ecuador. My clinic is now a small hospital and the majority of my medical staff is Cuban or Cuban trained. The Che portrait is long gone but his spirit is always present in the clinic.

In Ecuador, and many other countries, people work in environments vastly different from ours. Their paradigm is one of repression, fear and government control. In the chapters that follow, I will try to capture some examples of the world in which they operate and how it affects their lives, thoughts and experience. The despair that lingers is overwhelming knowing that these countries are broken and the people who live there have no idea that there is another, better way of life. Their way of thinking is not their own for it is ingrained in them that the U.S. and capitalism are evil. Contrary thought or expression is not tolerated and envy enslaves them. Their countries have gone too far down the road of socialism and its patterns of thought are too strongly deep-rooted in beliefs that are nothing short of catastrophic. In fairness, because freedom in our own sense has never really been part of their history, the concepts are completely foreign to them. For them, there is no path to a better economic life.

In other parts of the world, capitalism has triumphed. I often think how ironic it is that at the time that much of the world is experiencing success with capitalism and standards of living are rising for millions, we seem to be losing our enthusiasm for it. Unfortunately, there are many here in the U.S. who think that socialism is a path we should follow, that everything should be equal. This is no longer harmless chatter but a very serious collective decision. At some point as we continue down this path, there may be no way back.

Let's examine one aspect of our paradigm. As you read this, millions of U.S. students are laboring under the simple idea that if they study and work hard to get good grades, they will benefit from their own success in future job opportunity. What could be simpler? We compete with each other and this is understood in our way of life. We simply assume that opportunity will open for the harder working student in a way that may not for others who choose a different direction in life. We are confident that our hard work and individual talent will move us farther in our chosen fields. We believe that it is imminently fair that hard work will bring professional and economic success. We also know that competition brings out the best in all of us. From this competition will emerge better students, with more ideas who will advance more in their chosen fields. The student studies on, confident that the system into which he or she will soon graduate will fairly value and reward his/her ambition. This is not the case in the countries where I work. Success is suspect, there are few or no jobs available and talent or hard work may have little to do with getting one.

We have dreams and the freedom to pursue them. This is as natural to our way of life as breathing. But in a socialist country, the system doesn't operate this way. A person's own particular talents may not matter much at all because; their path and position in life is defined by the government; their major in college is selected by the government; their ability to get a job is based, not on their capability, talent or hard work, but on a connection they have to the current minister of.... you name it, they are limitless. It matters little that these functionaries change every few months due to political instability. Your job security will last only as long as they do.

I have worked in hospitals where the directors were simply political functionaries who knew nothing of health care and who changed every few months. It was no wonder that the hospitals were deplorable. I remember a young burn victim named Santa Banchon, from the island of Puna off the coast of Ecuador. We treated her on five occasions to allow her to move her head which was fused to her shoulder by her burns. We became quite close as she endured many painful surgeries over several years. The last time I saw her, she was recovering in a broken public hospital in Machala, Ecuador. She lay alone in significant pain next to a large window that, unbelievably, had no glass in it. There were insects on her and when it rained, it rained on her. Seeing her like this, I admit that I cried there for a long time; not just for her but for the countless children like her who suffer in such terrible conditions. I do not want this for my country and these are images that cannot, nor will I allow them to, be erased from my mind.

Do you wonder why nothing lasts in socialist societies? Why the quality of work is so poor? Why the quality of buildings, construction materials and manufactured goods is so shabby? Why there is no innovation? It is simply because it doesn't matter. In the socialist paradigm there is nothing to be gained by working or studying harder, making a better product, or providing a better service. This is what the United Nations means by the widespread corruption that plagues the third world and why it acknowledges that this it is its most overwhelming obstacle. When I was that same studying student years ago, I took for granted that my own initiative and hard work would some day pay off; that I would control my own destiny; that the world held opportunity for me and would treat me fairly. It never occurred to me that it could be any other way. Now I know better and I despair for those who do not know freedom or opportunity; and for those here who still take it for granted.

The essence of freedom in an economic sense is in our ability to choose our own way, to make our own economic decisions, to pursue our own dreams and benefit from our own personal talent and hard work. Absolutely fundamental to this is the confidence that our laws and institutions recognize, protect and value our individual freedoms and the right we share to pursue our own happiness. Basic to all of this is the notion of competition, as I mentioned earlier. Competition and the free pursuit of our personal interests are, after all is said and done, the engine that makes Capitalism so powerful. This, in turn creates benefits for all of society. The philosopher Adam Smith called this the "Invisible Hand."

> "*Every individual necessarily labours to render
> the annual revenue of the society as great as he
> can. He generally neither intends to promote
> the public interest, nor knows how much he is
> promoting it ... He intends only his own gain,
> and he is in this, as in many other cases, led
> by an invisible hand to promote an end which
> was no part of his intention. Nor is it always*

11

the worse for society that it was no part of his intention. By pursuing his own interest he frequently promotes that of the society more effectually than when he really intends to promote it. I have never known much good done by those who affected to trade for the public good."

ADAM SMITH

When people believe they have better ideas and they are free to pursue them, they create better products and services, better solutions, better mousetraps, cars, computers, phones and things that inherently make our lives better. In this process, the result is as much about the person's life as it is about the product manufactured. Because of their efforts, people are more fulfilled and their lives have greater meaning and purpose. They innovate and experiment, take risk, invest money and benefit when they succeed. In so doing, they create wealth certainly for themselves but more importantly for society as a whole in the jobs, products and benefits they create. While contributing to the public good was not their original intent, it is the natural outcome. There are those who ridicule this concept but I can find in it nothing but self-evident truth. There is no evidence that any other system in the world can match ours in its power to create individual and collective wealth. And it is from this collective wealth that we can count the blessings of safe neighborhoods, beautiful public libraries, sound schools, quality hospitals, museums and the arts; all of the things that make the quality of our lives exceptional. The next time you hear someone speak against capitalism or ridicule the concept of the invisible hand, remember Steve Jobs who had exceptional ideas and the freedom to pursue them. Did he make a fortune for himself? Yes, of course he did. But in the process, he created countless jobs all over the world, generated unimaginable commerce, paid a mountain of taxes, and made all of our lives better with products we enjoy and benefit from. Many progressives miss the very essence of this process because, to them, wealth is fixed and must therefore be divided and shared fairly. Steve Jobs <u>created</u> wealth. He took nothing from another person. The wealth did not exist before him. And remember his contemporary, Bill Gates, whose wealth made possible the creation of a foundation that seeks to eradicate the worst of the world's diseases in its poorest countries. None of this is theoretical. It is real and multiplied out in millions of individuals and companies throughout our country that are the engine of our collective wealth and strength as a nation. Individual success leads to collective prosperity.

If you have been taught that prosperity is immoral, walk for 5 minutes in the vast slums of Guatemala City or visit the families and children that live in and around its infamous dump. If you come out alive and sane, you will know with certainty that what Adam Smith said in 1776 is still genuinely true today. You may then forego your moral indignation and accept that there is no moral superiority in gross, but nearly equal, poverty. Competition, a free marketplace and the freedom to compete and succeed create the wealth that benefits us all. Anyone who tells you otherwise is a fool.

HUMANITARIAN LIFE

I t was 17 years ago when I began working with foreign surgical teams organizing trips to Central and South America.
I have had the great fortune of being part of more than 20
such trips to Colombia, Paraguay, Guatemala and Ecuador.
My early experiences with these challenging and successful, but short-term, surgical missions resulted in a desire to
establish something more permanent; to put down roots
and try to create change from the inside in a more permanent way. This was the genesis of my Ecuadorian foundation, Fibuspam, and my medical clinic located in Riobamba,
Ecuador. My foundation and clinic, since their inception
in 2007, have provided medical care to tens of thousands of
children and adults throughout Ecuador. Our organization
has also become a powerful agent of hope and change for
the indigenous population of Chimborazo province which
has suffered great discrimination and hatred and is often denied access to any kind of health care. We work in an area
of great poverty and hopelessness with significant problems
with child abandonment, child labor and trafficking, abuse,
and malnutrition.

Our foundation provides medical services to the poor in four ways.

Our clinic in Riobamba, Clinica Fibuspam. In 2007, in the balcony of a Riobamba church, I opened a very small, one-room health clinic to serve the basic medical needs of local children. My simple vision then was to have the equivalent of a school nurse's office. How I underestimated the talents and dreams of my local partners and the unexpected joy and potential in empowering those who want to make a difference in the world.

One year later, we expanded the clinic to include dental care, a laboratory and a bathroom. In that small space, over the next two years, we provided care to over 5,000 children. In 2010, I purchased an adjacent property and transformed the structure into a one- story clinic facility with doctors' offices, a pharmacy, a dental clinic, a laboratory, kitchen, emergency room and waiting room. It was only a year later that we were able to add a second floor that became our surgical wing. On this floor we now have two fully equipped operating rooms, a recovery room, six patient beds, and a complete eye clinic. With the addition of a large diesel generator in early 2015, we completed the requirements for accreditation as an ambulatory surgical center. The facility is now proudly known as Centro Clinico Quirurgico Fibuspam. We are now able to treat hundreds of children and adults every week in multiple specialties and perform surgery nearly every day, including eye surgery. The amount of care we deliver is stunning and we are changing lives every single day.

Medical Caravans. Roughly every two weeks, our small army of staff and volunteer physicians organize what we call "caravanas" to bring medical care to remote Andean communities where people seldom or never see a doctor. Our caravanas provide dental and general medical care, lab tests and vision screenings. The patients receive their prescriptions and we provide all medicines. Because of the generous support for my organization, all of this care is at no cost. We typically treat 200-300 grateful children and adults at each caravan. These weekend missions are incredibly productive, rewarding and interesting and take us to remote locations throughout Ecuador including the Amazon. Our reputation is strong and we are trusted and welcome wherever we go. Most of these communities are extremely poor and we see more than our share of serious medical and other problems. I have seen communities completely empty of males between the ages of 16 and 50 because of the massive emigration out of Ecuador and from this region in particular. Since 2000, nearly 4 million people, 25% of the country's population, have fled the country for the U.S. and Europe.

Foreign Medical Teams. Several times a year, we host foreign surgical teams who provide free surgical care to the needy both at our clinic and at the local military hospital with which we have a strong relationship. These teams generally complete 200-300 surgeries per year. Fibuspam is an important and valuable resource to these teams because we have the experience, and in-country relationships to organize a successful trip in compliance with all Ecuadorian laws. Because of our extensive relationships throughout Ecuador, particularly in the indigenous communities, and the trust we have developed, we are able to identify and pre-screen patients to assure a successful and productive trip. Lastly, and importantly, we are able to provide the necessary patient follow-up care after the teams return to their home countries. In 2015, Fibuspam, on its own, organized its first two surgical missions performing eye surgery at two locations in Ecuador far from Riobamba.

Special/Emergency Care and Social Services. Quite often, we come into contact with cases far too serious and complex for our resources and beyond the abilities and equipment of local doctors and hospitals. Cases include severe burns, other devastating accidents and rare medical conditions. In almost all cases, not only is the expertise not available but, even if it were, the people we serve have no money to pay for the care. Over our many years, our foundation has developed valuable relationships that can provide hope for these families. One example is our close relationship with the great Shriners Hospitals here in the U.S. Shriners has an office and staff in Ecuador and we work closely with them. Fibuspam provides all the logistical work to get the patients out of Ecuador and into the U.S. including visas and passports and other permissions, we counsel with the families and provide host support while the patient is in the U.S. receiving care. In the first quarter of 2016, we had three children here in the U.S. receiving extraordinary care and a chance to live normal lives.

As you can imagine, our work is challenging but powerfully rewarding.

In my first book, "To the Least of these My Brothers," I shared a heartwarming collection of essays that capture the intensity of the emotion, cultural discovery, challenges and rewards in providing humanitarian medical care to third-world children. I will to share two of these stories and others with you in this book to better illustrate the problems we face, how we get involved and the reality of life not just in Ecuador but throughout Central and South America.

SONIA CHAVEZ

O ver my many years working in Ecuador, I have had the honor of working closely with a number of humanitarians and in them I have many heroes. A close friend of mine, Marliza Garcia, is one of them. Marliza works for the government in the area of child labor and sexual abuse. I hadn't spoken with her in some time but to my surprise, one day an email from her popped up in my in-box. She told me that she was working with a young girl named Sonia Chavez who lived outside of the city of Cuenca, Ecuador. She said that Sonia was a victim of child labor. She was 12 years old. Her parents were forcing her to work nights in a "camal," or slaughterhouse. What job she did there or the conditions she worked in, thankfully, I never knew. How she worked nights and got up for school the next day is also a mystery to me. This was childhood for Sonia and it is a sad byproduct of the gross poverty faced by many families in this broken country and others. Marliza explained that she had rescued Sonia and, with local authorities, was working with the parents who were breaking international law by forcing their young daughter to work. I kept reading the email and the real reason for her letter soon became clear. When she got to know Sonia, Marliza saw that she had a microtia, that is, her right ear had never formed on the outside. It was a significant deformity and one that Sonia was certain to live and suffer with, probably alone, for the rest of her life. Life can be cruel to women in South America. I have seen women with young children abandoned by their husbands because of a minor skin problem; teenage girls with untreated primary cleft lips; young girls with STD's from sexual abuse by their fathers; countless women who are told not to speak by their husbands because they have nothing to say; young girls with broken bones that were never treated and never healed correctly. Marliza wanted to know if we could help Sonia. You can probably guess that, as it turned out...we could.

For years I have worked with a plastic surgeon from Guayaquil named Miguel. Miguel is a great humanitarian who has worked in every hospital in Ecuador helping the poor. I asked him if he would be willing to travel to Riobamba and do the first stage of a microtia repair for Sonia. It is an interesting and challenging surgery that is part science and part artistry. It involves two surgeries at once. One, preparing the ear area for the insertion of a prosthetic structure and two, the creation of the ear structure from cartilage removed from the ribs. We arranged and paid for Sonia's travel to Riobamba and Miguel brought his nurse and anesthesiologist from Guayaquil. The surgery was completed in our own operating room and I was blessed to be present and to meet Sonia. One year later, the scene repeated itself and the second stage of her surgery was completed. Sonia returned home still bandaged on a six- hour bus ride in the new clothes we had bought for her. I will never see her again but my hope for her is some happiness and love from someone, someday in her life.

ENVY AND ITS POLITICS

"Envy's a coal comes hissing hot from hell."

PHILIP JAMES BAILEY

Extreme poverty carries with it unique psychological effects, the most powerful of which is persistent and poisonous envy. When a person has nothing, he resents anyone with more than he has and consumes himself with hatred for others. It is the most difficult aspect of working in a poor, socialist country and its cruelty can be shocking. There is a man in the community in which I work that I know well. Because he was so poor, I once paid for emergency surgery for his wife. I supported the living expenses of his son for two years while the son studied medicine in Cuba. I paid the son's air-fare when he reurned home at Christmas to visit his family. Sadly, along with others, this man regularly lies about me in the community. He spreads rumors that I profit from my clinic. Over the last 9 years, I have invested hundreds of thousands of dollars to build, equip and staff what is now an accredited surgical center. We have provided free medical care, surgery and prescriptions to tens of thousands of children and adults throughout Chimborazo Province and beyond. My staff, volunteers and I joke about the "profits' we derive from our work when we are together, each one of us knowing only the profound joy of helping those that are suffering or in need. I often say that it is one thing to know that suffering exists but quite another to hold it in your hands and know that you can make it better. Nevertheless, I am left with another young man who runs a nearby school populated by children for whom I have provided free medical care for five years. He tells the children that I am a bad person and repeats the lie that I am profiting from my clinic. The children of course, believe him. I cannot describe how hurtful this is to me and to others who have to endure such rumors and lies. Such is the potent effect of envy.

"The spirit of envy can destroy; it can never build."

MARGARET THATCHER

When people are not free to prosper, they must find other ways to acquire goods. They learn to wear many masks to get what they need. For this reason, I have learned I have to be careful and to be suspect of everyone. This is not my nature nor is it the norm for most Americans. Here in the U.S., we are generally a trusting people and in this, we are very fortunate. We go about our business trusting that the person with whom we are dealing is driven by the same self-interest as we are. In my humanitarian work, I never know who to trust, what they really want from me or what they say to others about me behind my back. The reality of this is appalling and is a predictable bi-product in the Socialist paradigm. Envy consumes people and can cause them to act with a loathsome cruelty. When one does not respect success or wealth in others, the only response is to criticize, attack and tear the person down. We are a fortunate people to go through our daily lives with self-respect, trusting others, respecting their success and being treated fairly in return. This is the way life is in the Paradigm of Freedom.

> *"In recompense, envy may be the subtlest, perhaps I should say the most insidious, of the seven deadly sins."*

JOSEPH EPSTEIN

Because of the prosperity we enjoy, we are free to be a charitable people. We don't think about it, it's our way of life. We are not generally suspicious of those who offer charity. We value benevolence and are not normally threatened if someone is more benevolent than we are. We are free to make such decisions for ourselves. Our altruism supports and perpetuates the things we value in our societies: our libraries, hospitals, colleges, etc. In corrupt societies, charity is suspect. Perhaps because people are desperate to find any way to acquire things, the worst motives are always assumed when someone has something. There is little or no charity and, as a result, nothing of value endures. When I travel, I am always shocked to realize that people truly have no idea why I do the things I do. They ask me all the time. I answer them but my explanation does not resonate; and they will believe anything that is said about me.

> *"Worth begets in base minds, envy;*
> *in great souls, emulation."*

HENRY FIELDING

I have come to expect the attacks and rumors and, luckily, I live far from the daily rumor mill. The one who suffers most is my executive director in Riobamba. He is an immensely talented and courageous man who stands out in his community as an entrepreneur. He has excellent business sense and a respect for freedom and the importance of capital. Rising as he has from a particularly poor indigenous population subject to significant and harsh discrimination, he is someone I admire greatly. He is an exceptional person and I wonder how he came to have these qualities. Because of his success, our friendship and close collaboration, he is constantly the subject of nasty rumors and lies. He is often betrayed by the very people he thought were his closest friends. When he and I speak about it, he is saddened and embarrassed by the behavior of his people. I'm not sure how he and his family endure it.

A Humanitarian's Defense of Capitalism

I was once asked to speak to a large private high school by its founder who admired the United States and its freedom and opportunity. He asked me to focus specifically on the concept of freedom and the notion that one person's success does not come at the expense of another's; that it is fair that if someone works harder than another that they should earn more; that creating wealth does not mean that you are taking something from someone else; that someone honest and successful should be emulated. It was humbling and remarkable talking to the students who could not wrap their minds around what I was sharing with them because these concepts were so foreign, so new to them. The questions could have gone on for hours. While I was glad for the experience, I left the school knowing that a very different mentality awaited them right outside the door; a paradigm in which they are trapped.

Here in the U.S. education system, my observation is that there is at best apathy and at worst antagonism toward our own economic system. A surprising number of people I speak to know little or nothing about how our economy actually works but they are quite certain that they disapprove of it. Their disdain is palpable and travels fast on social media. Those who learn anything about capitalism and socialism in their high school and college classes hear the theoretical, technical aspects of each and the differences may end up seeming somewhat trivial. But the choice between democratic capitalism and socialism is a very serious one. They are not simply two paths to the same place. Garrison Keilor had it right when he said, "You can't arrive at the truth by adding up both sides and dividing by two. Truth is out there. You have to look for it." I have tried to illustrate here the destructive paradigm of socialist economic life. A socialist mentality poisons relationships and communities and saps the energy and dignity out of life and work.

"There is not a passion so strongly rooted
in the human heart as envy."

RICHARD BRINSLEY SHERIDAN

Perhaps it is not surprising that a person living in poverty should be plagued with envy. But this is where education plays a vital role. People can be taught a different paradigm. They can be taught that they are not doomed to poverty; that we all have unique talents in varied amounts; that some will succeed more than others and that someone else's success does not diminish another's; that financial success need not be immoral; that the concept of a growing pie is true. I could go on.

My main point though, as it relates to envy, is much more serious and relates to us here in the U.S. As I said, I believe envy may be the strongest and most destructive emotion we share as humans. It is also the easiest to manipulate. The paradigm of socialism springs from envy and over centuries, politicians, dictators and leftist despots have used envy to gain and hold power.

"Envy is the art of counting the other fellow's blessings instead of our own."

HAROLD COFFIN

There is simply no easier way to divide a people or build a political power base than by reminding them as often as possible, that someone, or some group, has more than they do. Worse, planting the notion that this someone, or group, has something <u>at their expense</u> is the icing on the cake. Naturally, the politician and his/her party have just the solution to make things "fair." Listen carefully to what progressive politicians say and you will learn a great deal. As we have seen in Venezuela, and what plays out ad nauseum in other countries, a determined populist can completely ruin a country in less than two decades. It is envy's seed they are planting and they are poisonous. A population consumed by envy will be the ruin of any nation.

Where we stand on this subject in the U.S. in 2016 is extremely troubling. Over the last several years a new political glossary has appeared that is beginning to define us in a new and troubling way. Much of it is based on misinformation and outright lies and, sadly, many Americans simply accept it. The comments about business owners in my Foreword are the gold standard but many politicians and citizens are learning to speak the language. The seeds of envy and division are being planted and are taking root. Scores of deceptive phrases trip off the tongues of politicians and the media with nary a blink. *"The richest 1%." "The basic bargain at the heart of our economy has frayed." "Those at the top." "Different set of rules." "Level the playing field." "Income inequality." "Fairness". "Fair share." "Fat cats."* This dangerous new vocabulary is all around us. In a later section of this book I address some of the falsehoods that underlie this destructive new vocabulary. Its audacity is only exceeded by its deception. This is a drastic change in political discourse in our country that will do us great harm. It is the siren song of socialism and a generation is listening. Are you willing to acquiesce to leaders who fabricate unfairness to incite populist division and grow political power? The way to attain more prosperity for all Americans is not by manufacturing falsehoods and promoting the notion that the business community is a bunch of thieves who prosper at your expense. This is reprehensible, irresponsible and dangerous. It is a fool's errand to spend our energy comparing ourselves to others, crafting legislation that pretends to create more equality but damages our country, and growing government to pursue the impossible goal of economic justice. Better that we attend to the economic system from which we derive our collective prosperity and deal with the real economic problems that hold us <u>all</u> back and prevent us all from succeeding.

A Humanitarian's Defense of Capitalism

*"The leading object (of government) is to elevate
the condition of men — to lift artificial weights
from all shoulders — to clear the paths of laudable
pursuit for all — to afford all an unfettered
start, and a fair chance, in the race of life."*

ABRAHAM LINCOLN

To use an analogy, it is so much easier for a child to believe in the tooth fairy than to understand the science of dental care. Likewise, it is almost impossible not to believe that a utopia of economic equality is possible and that we simply need bigger government to make it work. There is no evidence that a socialist model of a more just society has ever worked anywhere. It has not. The danger is that it is nearly impossible for the complex reality of capitalism to compete with the fantasy of a socialist utopia. But despite a history of socialist failure, and more unfolding today before our eyes, why are so many receptive to a socialist fairy tale and open to those who portray capitalism as something contemptible?

It is often said that the perfect is the enemy of the good. Let's agree that capitalism is not a perfect economic system. But it is as close to it as the world has ever known. Capitalism provides a potent economic engine consistent with our framework as a free people. It is succeeding in raising standards of living for millions around the world. True, its excesses are often hard to understand and those who do succeed have a responsibility to act honestly and responsibly. But as we've discussed, these excesses are usually due to human fault and not the system itself. Do you think there is no greed or corruption in a socialist system? Indeed, these countries are drowning in them.

Its effects are much more pervasive and destructive because of the massive power of government in socialist countries. The socialist path leads to a world of tyranny, financial failure, hopelessness, poverty and corruption. This is not theoretical. Speaking of the Soviet era in her own country, Nobel Prize winner Svetlana Alexievich wrote,

"I reconstruct the history of that battle, its victories and its defeats. The history of how people wanted to build the Heavenly Kingdom on earth. Paradise! In the end, all that remained was a sea of blood and millions of ruined lives. This is important because arguments about socialism have not died down. A new generation has grown up with a different picture of the world and many young people are reading Marx and Lenin again... They all come from the same place-socialism. There are many idealists among them. Romantics. Today they are sometimes called slavery romantics. Slaves of utopia."

In his beautiful poem, *Desiderata*, Max Ehrmann wrote:

"If you compare yourself with others, you may become vain and bitter;
For always there will be greater and lesser persons than yourself."

Envy is a trap; we should avoid it and be wary of those who would put us in it for their own political gain. After all, we all have a choice. We can spend our time comparing ourselves to others in bitterness and envy; or we can use what resources and gifts we have to better ourselves and the world. Our economic table is set and, more than at any time in our history, there is a seat at it for everyone. You can spend your time railing at its imperfections if you want; or you can sit down with others and make something happen. Save your anger and pity for those in the world who have no table at all.

WHY SOCIALISM FAILS

*"Socialism is a philosophy of failure, the creed of
ignorance and the gospel of envy. Its inherent
virtue is the equal sharing of misery."*

WINSTON CHURCHILL

As we said, a capitalist system springs directly from the
notion of freedom, a notion fundamentally embedded
in our lives as Americans. We are free to make decisions
about our economic lives based on our talents, resources and
ambition. Resources are allocated among participants operating freely in a free market. The role of government is to
insure that rights are protected, that everyone can enter the
marketplace of talent and ideas and that the rule of law is
applied fairly to all. In a socialist system, exactly who makes
the economic decisions? In the absence of freedom, who decides who gets what, who wins, who loses, what prices are, or
what level of profit or income is fair? The answer is government and here we have a completely different paradigm. In
a socialist system, power by definition resides in government.
The individual gives up his or her freedom for the promise

of a more just outcome that a central authority will deliver. And so, government sets itself to the task of managing everything; a task that becomes more absurd even as its impossibility becomes more evident.

Recently in Venezuela, which 20 years ago was a bright light of democracy and economic success in South America, the socialist government actually outlawed inflation. Imagine it! In 1995 the "Bolivarian Revolution" brought socialist dictator Hugo Chavez to power. Over several years, power and ownership were concentrated in the government, the constitution and courts were perverted, basic freedoms were curtailed, thousands were jailed and radical socialist economic policies were enacted. Despite having the world's largest oil reserves, the country soon became an economic disaster with widespread shortages, unemployment, hopelessness, violence, brutal repression and fear. Caracas, its capital, is now considered the most violent city in the world. The worse things get, the more central control is applied. (The beatings will continue until the morale improves!) Not long ago, inflation there topped 275% per year and its currency has lost 93% of its value in the last two years. The currency literally loses significant value overnight. If you were a storeowner selling refrigerators and you were lucky enough to acquire one to sell, because of the wild inflation you would have to raise your price each day just to get back what you paid. But the laws of nature and physics don't apply in socialist utopias and the government passed a law making it illegal to raise prices. Government agents actually monitor prices in shops and supermarkets and a violation will land you in jail. Thus, the government is mandating that their merchants lose money. With astonishing ignorance, the country's new Finance Minister recently declared that *"Inflation doesn't exist in real life."*

But what do truth or reality matter in the pursuit of fairness and economic justice and the struggle against the privileged elite? And so, the private sector shrinks and shrinks as government uses more and more resources on bureaucracy for, you guessed it, the good of the people. As the private sector shrinks, the government must tax more to maintain its control and power. Thus, the engine of the national car becomes weaker and weaker while the load it is tasked with gets larger and larger. Eventually, the engine stalls and societal chaos erupts. Everyone wonders what happened. By then, the people have long forgotten that there used to be an engine in the car; that the engine was what got them from one place to another. But the engine was neglected and the people became apathetic about its maintenance and care. And so today in Venezuela, as they stand daily in long lines hoping to buy milk and bread as their government collapses, you might hear them say, "We had better things to worry about like fairness and economic justice, right? We really showed it to those fat cats, didn't we? Well, didn't we?"

As I have illustrated, this is not theoretical. Some other examples may help you. In socialist countries, working for the government is considered a good job. It matters not a whit that there is no productivity whatsoever in the job, or that the job serves no particular purpose. Government is power and jobs are power. Bureaucracy is rampant and it sucks the life out of everything. The population spends unbelievable amounts of time traveling and waiting in lines to comply with the most nonsensical rules that govern every aspect of public life. Imagine that you live in Boston and you constantly have to drive 4-5 hours to New York to accomplish even the simplest bureaucratic tasks. I know this because my staff is constantly traveling on buses to complete the most mundane, useless tasks. By the way, robbery is rampant on the buses and I worry for them constantly. Such is life in utopia. When government runs everything, laws become incredibly complex. The laws also change constantly and because no one really knows what they are, officials make them up giving rise to rampant corruption and disrespect for the law. In the absence of freedom, government becomes pervasive. So much to manage! And because the countries are unstable (remember, no engine) the governments change often creating a constant parade of functionaries who don't know their jobs. Through it all, the people must comply and thus the talents and productive capacity of a population of talented people are wasted. The people are indeed largely equal and they share in their frustration and misery equally. In Paraguay, I was surprised to find that the government assigns a number to every single desk, chair, table and piece of equipment in the country no matter how basic. How many people does it take to manage this useless inventory? Can you imagine for one moment the waste this represents? No one has a good job but at least someone is keeping track of the chairs in the cafeteria! Care to start a business? Good luck! It may take you a year or more to accomplish the tasks you must complete for the maze of ministries that will approve and govern your business. Be careful not to speak badly of those in power, by the way, there may be a slight delay.

In the United States, we have this quaint tradition of giving bonuses to those who excel in their jobs. It is a tangible reward to recognize outstanding work and is a positive, motivating factor that fosters competition, creativity and productivity. Employees are free to strive for such bonuses and employers are free to pay them or not as they choose. In the countries where I travel, employers pay bonuses too, but only because the government tells them to. Paying a bonus is compulsory. Every employee gets the same "bonus" regardless of the quality of his/her work. This may seem trivial but it is at the heart of the socialist paradigm. It does not matter one bit whether you are the worst or the best employee. Why would anyone strive to excel, exercise any ambition, innovate or try to improve the business? The answer is, they wouldn't.

Another example of the contrast in paradigms is illustrative. In the US, it is considered extremely bad manners to ask a person what he or she makes at their job. This is considered very private and it should be. We are all different and here in the US we are free to compete, to work and study harder, to work more hours if we wish, to innovate and take more responsibility if we desire. In this way, our earnings differ based on many factors and our relationships with our employers and how they view our value is private. This is fundamental to our way of life. In stark contrast, in a socialist country, an employee signs a monthly payroll summary that clearly shows what everyone is being paid. The government requires it. In this system, things better be equal or there will be hell to pay. Everyone knows what everyone makes. Envy takes care of the rest. The result, as I have explained, is an environment where ambition is suspect, envy, rivalry and lies are rampant and there is little incentive to excel or innovate. I have had exemplary employees that I have wanted to reward but have always been frustrated by a government mandated payroll system that virtually guarantees mediocrity. Ironic that a system designed to insure fairness does so much interpersonal and economic damage. Such is life in an economic utopia built on boneheaded ideas.

The socialist paradigm impacts every aspect of life; the quality of life, the quality of work and the will to compete and succeed. When an oppressive and omnipresent government controls everything in the pursuit of economic justice and income equality, the meaning and purpose of individual lives, choices, responsibilities and livelihoods is diminished. The inevitable decline of prosperity and capital takes its toll on public services, infrastructure and the general quality of, well, everything. It is not a pretty sight. Society slowly takes on a shabby, hopeless sense where masses of people surge in enormous waves of desperation in search of survival. Life in a socialist paradigm lacks any sense of permanence or the sense of security, control and collective prosperity that we are so used to. When people give up control of their lives, they get what government gives them and nothing more. To aspire for more is not an option. In what has to be the most bland, bureaucratic understatement of all time, the World Bank published the following about the reality of income equality:

> "An excessively equal income distribution
> can be bad for economic efficiency.
> Take, for example, the experience of
> socialist countries where deliberately
> low inequality (with no private profits
> and minimal differences in wages and
> salaries) deprived people of the incentives
> needed for their active participation in
> economic activities-for diligent work and
> vigorous entrepreneurship. Among the
> consequences of socialist equalization
> of incomes were poor discipline and low
> initiative among workers, poor quality and
> limited selection of goods and services, slow
> technical progress, and eventually, slower
> economic growth leading to more poverty."
> Beyond Economic Growth-An Introduction
> to Sustainable Development

> TATYANA P. SOUBBOTINA-2004

A Humanitarian's Defense of Capitalism

Keep this quote in mind the next time you take your child or grandchild to your beautiful local library, or visit your child at a great university, or visit a loved one in a well-equipped, clean hospital, or call the police or an ambulance in an emergency and they actually come in minutes. The socialist countries where I work have none of these things. Sooner than we think, I fear, neither will we.

Yvonne Macias

(From *"To the Least of These My Brothers"* by Paul Martel)

To love another person is to see the face of God.
Les Miserables

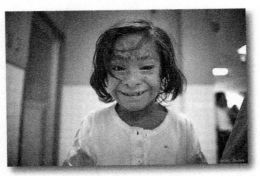

© 2006 Derek Dudek

The story of little Yvonne Macias from Guayaquil, Ecuador embodies many special aspects of my medical trips and ends, like so many of my experiences, in a strange mix of sadness and warmth. The first day of any trip is screening day. Hundreds of parents and families travel great distances by bus, by foot or by burro to our host hospitals in the hope that their children will be selected for surgery. It is always a chaotic frenzy of bi-lingual communication, professional collaboration, hope, desperation and often disappointment.

Early one screening day at the children's hospital in Guayaquil, I noticed a mother with her young daughter in the crowd. The little girl had a shocking, severe skin condition and it was difficult to look at her. I had much to do and though I was curious, I kept to my work. A little later, my good friend and our host, Ecuadorian humanitarian Zorayda Figueroa, came into my office, took my hand and led me into the hallway. She marched me up to that same child and demanded that I help her. She said that no doctors in Guayaquil would help her, that the hospital didn't want her there, and that she didn't care what they said. "Please," she said, "bring her to the doctors and ask them to help her." I am not one to argue with Zorayda and she now had me holding this poor child's hand in mine. Yvonne's appearance was somewhat horrific. The skin all over her body was dark, leather-like, scaly and peeling. Her hair and her clothes were filthy. Zorayda told me that people thought she had suffered radiation from nuclear testing in the Pacific. She told me that Yvonne was unable to close her eyes because of the hardness of her skin. She said that insects often fed on the dead skin that constantly peeled off her body. On our medical trips it is not unusual to see rare and bizarre medical conditions and the experience is always sobering and upsetting. I led Yvonne down the crowded hall to our general surgeons Joe and Jon. They were quite curious and agreed to examine her. The consensus was that she had a very rare skin condition called Ictheosis. They said there was little that could be done for her but that they might be able to make it possible for her to close her eyes. They said that she would soon go blind from the dryness of not being able to blink and moisten her eyes. Their plan was to graft a small strip of skin below each eye which would allow them to close. The only problem was that there were few, if any, suitable donor sites on her body where they could get some good skin to graft to her eyes. Nevertheless, they said they would try. Zorayda was thrilled and when I think of her and that episode I am reminded of the Biblical phrase, "As you did it to the least of these my brethren, you did it unto me." Quite simply, doing for the least of her brethren is Zorayda's life.

© 2006 Derek Dudek

I led Yvonne and her mother back to my "office" and began to get their information into the computer. Zorayda ran off joyfully continuing her tireless advocacy for children.

By now, Yvonne and I were becoming buddies. She was very friendly, curious and playful like any 6 year old. She walked around my desk staring at my computer. I was quite drawn to her but afraid to touch her at the same time. At that moment, I clearly remember thinking, "Paul, caring for children like Yvonne is what you came all this way for, isn't it!" "What are you waiting for?" I picked her up and put her on my lap and the look on her face told me that that didn't happen very often. For the next hour, she sat with me helping me type names into the computer. We played and laughed and a strong bond quickly developed. I got hopelessly behind in my work and finally had to track her mother down and get her on her way. They apparently had nowhere else to go but the hospital, and Yvonne continued to peek in at me throughout the afternoon and our friendship continued to grow. It wasn't her skin I was seeing anymore. It was the normal, playful, gentle child inside that I was beginning to love. Because of the type of procedure and her age, Yvonne's surgery was scheduled for the afternoon of our last day and this detail bears upon this story.

The last day of any medical trip is unique and important in many ways. It is a day of completion. Most surgeries are finished and the children are recovered and leaving the hospital. Parents are saying emotional goodbyes, and though they may have nothing, they bring touching gifts of flowers, eggs, fruit, cuy (guinea pig), and hand-made crafts. There are meetings with the hospital staff to settle up bills, track down lost items, distribute leftover supplies, review successes and problems, pack and discuss the next trip. There are dignitaries to meet, wanting to share formal expressions of community gratitude. There are reporters and television people to talk with. The last day of a trip is also one of physical and emotional exhaustion after days with little sleep, endless hours in the hospital, negotiation, crisis, problem solving, heart-wrenching decisions and conversations, brilliant successes, disappointing failures and sometimes tragedies. For everyone, it is a day of goodbyes; a day of intense friendship between nurses and doctors from very different places and cultures who suddenly realize that they have shared a unique and precious experience; that together they have accomplished something remarkable. They also realize that their time together is over and that they may never see each other again. The afternoon of the last day is always very special to me. I enjoy wandering around the hospital watching people sharing gifts, shaking hands, hugging, laughing, sharing pictures of children, giving away scrubs and I inevitably conclude that life just can't be any better than it is at those moments. For a trip's Administrator, my usual role, the afternoon can present some free time. The operating schedule is nearly complete; there are no more children to track down, no more new children to screen, no more preparations to make or schedules to print, and no more medicines or fluids to chase after. It was in this emotional environment that Yvonne, our last case, presented herself for her surgery.

© 2006 Derek Dudek

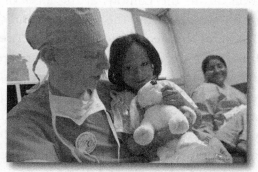

© 2006 Derek Dudek

She arrived with her mother quite early and I was grateful that I had the time to spend with her. I helped to get her changed into her gown and brought her into the small office we were using as a waiting room. I held her tightly while a nurse put the IV line into her little arm which, because of the condition of her skin, was difficult and upsetting to her. We sat together on the couch and, to calm her down a little, I took out some books in Spanish I had brought and began to read to her. I wondered if anyone ever read to this poor child and she seemed to enjoy it so much. Time passed and as I read she began to fall asleep. Soon, this precious child was fast asleep on my lap and I saw for the first time that she slept with her eyes wide open. This affected me deeply and I stared at her wondering how she could sleep like that, where she had slept the night before, if she lived on the street, if she had any friends or toys and what life was really like for her. I looked around, alone in the unusual quiet of that room; at the bustle out in the hallway; at the faces of my friends rushing by the window. And the memories and the joys and the exhaustion of the week suddenly washed over me like a huge, soft wave. I looked down again at Yvonne quietly sleeping. I stared at her face, her eyes and her awful skin and was overcome with sorrow for her. I was, as we say today, having a moment, and I was having trouble keeping from crying. Suddenly, at that very moment, through the door burst a glamorous television news reporter and her cameraman. Knowing I was free, Zorayda had sent her to me for an interview. In seconds, the cameraman had his light on and his camera pointing at me. The smiling reporter shoved a microphone in my face and said brightly in Spanish, "So, how do you feel right now?" Well, at that moment, Paul Martel from Simsbury, Connecticut couldn't have said much of anything about the way he felt or anything else for that matter. At that moment he did not feel very good. And he stared at the reporter, holding Yvonne in his arms, tears running down his face for the sorrow in which so many of the world's children live and he said nothing.

I often think back at what the reporter must have thought at that moment. She probably thought I was crazy. But as luck would have it, Zorayda was watching the whole thing from outside the room and came in to rescue me. She took over the interview as only she could and gave me some time to collect my thoughts. We completed the interview together and soon Yvonne was awake and being led to the OR for her surgery. I haven't seen her or her mother since we said good-bye in recovery after her surgery. I'm told that her eyes close beautifully and I often think of her and the many other children whose lives I've had the pleasure of touching.

© 2006 Derek Dudek

DEMOCRATIC SOCIALISM

The term Democratic Socialism has become popular around the world. Many countries, like ours, have adopted socialist components in their otherwise capitalist systems. In a larger sense, the term defines a new political paradigm that is more advanced in the U.S. than you might think. Most progressive candidates now publically identify as Democratic Socialists. But the name is quite simply a contradiction in terms. It is an impossibility. Democracy is a political system based on individual freedom and the right of a people to determine its own direction and elect its own leaders. The right to vote is at the core of the individual freedoms we enjoy. Socialism, in an economic sense, is the absence of freedom. It is the abdication of individual freedom, choice and responsibility to an autocracy that acts with absolute power and without consent. Despite the contradiction, Democratic Socialism has, amazingly, become part of our political vocabulary. Despite its absurdity, we accept the idea. How can this be? The answer is simple. It makes us feel better. It makes us think we can have the fairy tale of socialistic equality and keep our individual rights in the bargain. We can't. Rather than act responsibly and face the realities of spending and debt limits, we fool ourselves that the two can coexist; that we can be both free and unfree at the same time. This act of collective denial and delusion may at first seem subtle but it is evidence that we are well down the path of socialism. We just prefer not to admit it. We're old enough to know that there is no Santa Claus but we're not quite ready to give up the presents.

A quick look around the world is instructive and we can divide the march of Democratic Socialism into two categories. Neither has a good ending. First, we have the countries that identified as Democratic Socialist systems years before us. These are countries that are still in the collective denial stage. They are decidedly socialist but still pretend to be free. Two examples are Greece and Spain that still function as legitimate democracies. They have multiple parties, a free press and open elections. Both countries are failing. The problem at this stage is that the slow progression of denial has imperceptibly transformed their political vocabulary and landscape until, while they may have two or more political parties, they all speak from the far left of the political spectrum. It is, after all, what the people want to hear. In their case, the change did not happen overnight. It never does. They did not wake up one morning and collectively decide to become socialists. It is a generational, slow process of denial, apathy and irresponsibility. The national dialogue becomes not how to achieve national prosperity but which party can provide the most public benefit while still keeping up the charade. It is often said that a republic will endure until politicians realize they can bribe the people with their own money. The fallacy of the term Democratic Socialism is part of that bribe and we are fools to accept it. When this stage is reached, any politicians who try to state the obvious and instill fiscal discipline are now so far out of the mainstream that they are unelectable. Maintaining political power always trumps policy to advance the public good and so the process moves forward to its inevitable conclusion. The people want what they want and they will delude themselves that it is possible until, well...until it's not. In countries like Spain and Greece, and many others, we are looking at countries that are dying economically. They are helpless to stop it. Witness the massive street protests in Greece; a bankrupt people demanding benefits they know they cannot afford. "Give us what we want or we'll shoot ourselves!" This is not to be taken lightly. Their demise has very dire and real consequences for the millions of people who live there and for the European Union of which they are members and from whom they have borrowed billions. In a similar vein, you may not know that in 1998-99, the banking system in Ecuador and its currency, the Sucre, failed. Imagine waking up one morning and learning that your entire life savings is gone. This is what happened to millions of Ecuadorians and the same has happened to other countries around the world. In a sad and ironic contradiction, while Ecuador has adopted our U.S. dollar as their national currency, because their own currency failed, they rail at the U.S. for its imperialist intrusion. It is a political necessity and always works. Never underestimate the usefulness of anti U.S. rhetoric and, of course, a generous dose of envy, to maintain power.

The second category of Democratic Socialist nations are nations that are actually fully communist but pretend to be democracies. Countries such as Venezuela and Russia come to mind. In order to appear legitimate on the world stage and participate as members of various international forums and trade groups, they maintain a pathetic charade that only underscores the illegitimacy of their utopias. In each, the state owns all media and news outlets and controls the flow of information, including all political propaganda. The state uses intimidation to control voters and main opposition candidates have an uncanny record of winding up dead or in jail. The power of the State in communist systems is absolute and, despite the feeble attempts to appear otherwise, the people have no fundamental freedoms. Yet, the leaders of these countries, with straight faces, refer to themselves as Democracies.

Socialism implies, indeed demands, the very opposite of freedom in economic life. One gives up the right to make personal economic decisions to a larger, ultimately totalitarian authority under the theory that that authority will make collective decisions that will better serve society. The two approaches cannot coexist. The reality is that, should we choose to take history and logic seriously, we will see a litany of tragic proof that socialism nearly always ends very badly. Adding the word Democratic in front of it does not change its nature or its destructive results. "It's OK," we say to ourselves, "we are still democratic." In my view, using the term is simply a way that a people pretend they are not making the irresponsible collective decisions they are making. It is beyond them to stop themselves and they are helpless to resist the myth of socialism. Democratic Socialism is nothing but a grand exercise in collective denial. Ask the Greeks.

The Nordic Model

With the emergence of a socialist as a legitimate presidential candidate, there has been much discussion about what is called the Nordic Model. Progressives often point to Denmark as a shining example of the possibilities of Socialism. You might be surprised to learn, however, that the Prime Minister of Denmark, Lars Rasmussen, does not welcome these comments and rejects the notion that his country follows a socialist model. Quite the contrary, he emphasizes Denmark's centuries old commitment to free market capitalism and its fundamental importance in Danish society. Denmark has a strong historical commitment to what they call the "social contract" and they are collectively willing to shoulder an extremely high tax burden to maintain it. They have strong, shared ideals as to the importance of providing health, education, a healthy lifestyle and secure retirement to all Danish citizens. The key to their success, however, is an equally strong commitment to the free market capitalism and free enterprise that makes the social contract possible. For over a century, they have nurtured exactly the marriage and balance that I advocate in this book. Weakening their economic model would threaten their entire way of life. Demonizing prosperity or economic success would be unthinkable in their paradigm because it would threaten the very fabric of a society in which they rightly take immense pride. They are a people that collectively value entrepreneurship, access to capital and above all, a productive population. As an aside, the influx of Middle Eastern refugees is an especially grave threat to Denmark because the scope and cost of their social benefits is so great and they rely on a highly educated and productive work force. They are a small country of less than six million people and uncontrolled immigration has the potential of upsetting what is a delicate balance. They are rightly protective of what they have built in the last 100 years. The Danes have learned that the social contract cannot exist without prosperity. This is not socialism at all but a sort of super commitment to the social good by way of an equally super commitment to a highly educated and productive population operating in the model of free market capitalism. The remarkable success Denmark has achieved in the world is not due solely to its national commitment to the social good but to the marriage of that commitment with the resources that make it possible. It is an admirable, and I suspect fragile, balance that any nation can aspire to; including ours.

The goals of the social good and economic prosperity need not be in opposition. Each goal is worthy and each relies on the other. The goals are complimentary and their marriage should be nurtured and protected. Destroying the economic system that makes social benefit possible is simply foolhardy. Our country is fast losing the balance and synergy that we have enjoyed for generations. Capitalism is not the cause of our decline. Capitalism, free markets and a strong economy are the keys to restoring our strength, paying for the social benefits we enjoy and, when we can afford it, building on them. The Danish know that the will alone to strengthen the social contract cannot make it so. We must learn as a people that destroying the engine that makes our society and communities strong, makes our lives meaningful and pays for the social benefits we enjoy is the road to national failure.

THE MORALITY OF WEALTH

*"The fundamental error of socialism is
anthropological. Socialism considers the
individual simply as an element, so that the
good of the individual is completely subordinated
to the socioeconomic mechanism...A person
who is deprived of something he can call
'his own,' and of earning a living through
his own initiative, comes to depend on the
social machine and those who control it.*

*In the Christian vision, the social nature
of man is not completely fulfilled in the
state but is realized in various intermediary
groups, beginning with the family and
including economic, social, political, and
cultural groups that stem from human
nature itself and have their own autonomy,
always with a view to the common good."*

THE ECONOMICS OF HUMAN
FREEDOM, JOHN PAUL II

The 1980's were heady times in Eastern Europe. The collapse of the Soviet Union brought tens of millions of people face to face with the notion of living in freedom; something that they yearned for but did not understand. After living under brutal repression for generations, this was no doubt a moment of great discomfort, doubt and fear. Karol Wojtyla (Pope John Paul II), from Poland, more than any other leader, was able to capture the essence of that moment and articulate the promise and profound moral basis for human and economic freedom. Speaking often to immense crowds teeming with anxious anticipation, his three simple words, "Be not afraid" guided a new generation into the paradigm of freedom. Putting religion aside, his fundamental message was that man is more than a faceless, soulless tool in a tyrannical mechanism seeking to impose collective equality. He explained that the true nature of man is manifested in his individual right to seek meaning, purpose and happiness in life; to express his individuality, realize his human potential and, through exercising his free will, live life with dignity. The human spirit is manifested in many forms of expression and association: artistic, cultural, political and civic. In economic terms, it means having a meaningful job, having something he can call his own, providing for his family, pursuing his dreams, and having something of his own to share with others. These are the things that give meaning to our lives and that fulfill us as human beings. By recognizing and respecting the human spirit, in this sense, there is a profound morality to freedom and free enterprise.

A Humanitarian's Defense of Capitalism

"We hold these truths to be self-evident:
that all men are created equal; that they
are endowed by their Creator with certain
unalienable rights; that among these are life,
liberty, and the pursuit of happiness."

THOMAS JEFFERSON

Listening to progressives talk about concepts such as wealth, affluence and profit is always strange to me because of the disdain they openly hold for them. I puzzle at this and come at it from a very different perspective. I would agree that the pursuit of wealth and profit for its own sake could lead to an empty existence. I agree we should aspire to higher values, and a sense of charity and compassion in the world. But why do so many assume that those who seek financial success aren't also aspiring as well to those higher values? I have worked for years with scores of professionals and physicians who do exactly that. I admire them and they inspire me. More importantly, as a humanitarian, I know that without resources, I can't help anyone. Without wealth, there is no charity. Without resources, there is no help to offer. My question to those who are "Occupying 'Wall St.'" (whatever they think that means), stopping traffic or shutting down commerce to protest free enterprise is this: Do you not see the millions of human beings who are risking and losing their lives for the freedom and opportunity you enjoy? Are you blind to this reality? Are you so sure you want to give up what so many yearn for and dream of? Perhaps you might consider using that opportunity and freedom in a positive way to actually create change in the world. Thanks to our freedoms and our economic system, you have the power to make something happen; to be the change you want to see in the world. Use it. While the majority of progressives may not be sitting in the rain in a New York park hoping for revolution, isn't it the case that their apathy in not defending our freedoms and free markets is leading to the same socialistic conclusion albeit at a slower pace? Over my career, I've worked with humanitarians who have saved lives, given people sight, eased the suffering of burn victims, repaired deformed lips, palates, ears and legs for boys and girls who can grow up with hope of a normal life. Does anyone think this is free? Without financial resources, without an economic framework that creates wealth, none of this would have happened. The success of my business and the invaluable moral support of my partners and employees have made unimaginable things possible. This is the model we should replicate and teach. This is the model that offers us our highest and best use as humans in both an economic and moral sense. Free enterprise makes this possible.

In our universities, and to some extent in our state legislatures, there is a popular movement today called "Social Entrepreneurism." The idea has significant merit and recognizes the realities of economic freedom and free enterprise that I have explained in this book. It is based on the notion that the "profits" generated by an enterprise need not necessarily be owned by individuals but can be owned by the public good in general. Thus, the movement's goals are to formulate and experiment with new business forms or entities whose legal owners are not individuals but a perpetual benefit for the social good. A successful example of this is the company Newman's Own, whose profit from the sale of its popular food products is donated to a variety of charities. It is a model that rightfully recognizes the unique power of free enterprise while legally mandating that its profits belong to the public good. Wesleyan University in Connecticut has its own Patricelli Center for Social Entrepreneurship founded by Robert and Margaret Patricelli. It is an exciting experiment in pairing activism with enterprise. Several states are experimenting with new forms of entities to facilitate the formation and perpetuity of such ownership structures. While I applaud such efforts, the concept implies an immorality to an individual profit motive that I do not endorse. I would also caution anyone studying or contemplating such enterprise, that the entrepreneurship, not the social, must come first. It is only when you have a successful enterprise that you have anything to share with the public good. That being said, I have nothing but respect for entrepreneurs and workers who seek to join in business together in the pursuit of a larger cause and a better world and I am yet again grateful for the freedom they have to follow their dreams.

Here I would like to share a story that speaks loudly to the subject of this book and to other subjects relevant to our time. Every word of it is true. To begin, let's take a walk down the main street of my town. You will see a large window to a popular lunch spot. A Latino man is there every day making the bread. He is from South America and like so many others like him, you see him but he is largely invisible. This is the story of this man, his wife and his daughter. We will call them Miguel, Celia and Ana.

Miguel lived with his family in South America, in a country that at the time was suffering after years of bitter struggle with leftist revolutionaries. There was little wealth, few jobs, but plenty of hopelessness and desperation. One of this couple's parents was suffering with cancer and Miguel and Celia were helpless and unable to provide care. They made the nearly impossible decision to leave their country and travel to the U.S. for a period of time to earn money to pay for medical care for their loved one. Celia, who was not deemed a flight risk at the U.S. Embassy in her country, was granted a tourist visa. As is usually the case, Miguel was not. Celia found the resources to buy an airline ticket to New York, settled in with relatives and found work, albeit illegally. We will come back to her. Miguel, who had no visa but was determined to be with his wife, faced a different, long and very dangerous journey to the U.S. At tremendous risk, he traveled by boat, train and truck through many countries finally arriving near the U.S.-Mexico border. Two days before his small group planned to cross the border, they were robbed. None were harmed but they lost everything they had, including their shoes. The next night, they were robbed again, by the same gang. Miguel describes being forced to his knees with guns to each side of his head. "Go ahead and kill me, " he told them. "I have nothing left. You have already taken everything I have." Thankfully, they let him go and the next day he crossed the border into the U.S. Somehow, he found his way to his wife. They each found work and began sending funds home for medical care.

But what of their two year-old daughter, Ana? As is often the case, she remained behind with Celia's sister while her parents worked in the U.S. Several months later and very far away from her parents, Ana was diagnosed with a serious congenital heart defect that, left untreated, would take her life. Not only did her parents not have the money to pay for treatment in their country, the health care system was not advanced enough to provide it. Terrified, Miguel and Celia desperately began seeking a way to save their daughter's life and it is here, miraculously, that our paths crossed. Somehow, they made a connection to a talented and generous pediatric cardiologist at a local children's hospital. This very special physician, humanitarian, and friend of mine, generously offered her help and the help of her hospital and pointed them to me for assistance in the legal and administrative matters to get the child to the U.S. for care. This was to prove challenging. The most important job in bringing a child to the U.S. for medical care is obtaining the various permissions for the child to leave his/her own country, including compliance with child trafficking laws, and obtaining a visa for the child to legally enter the U.S. for medical care. I made application for Ana through normal channels and a visa interview was scheduled for her in her country's capital. I did not expect any problems.

One afternoon, shortly after her interview, I received a phone call from the U.S. embassy in their country. "Paul," the agent said, "we are considering the application for Ana and we would like to grant the visa as requested. We have only one problem. We know that the child's mother has overstayed her original tourist visa and is in the U.S. illegally. Here is what we can do. If the mother returns to her country and presents herself to the embassy, we will grant her child a visa." In that conversation I was introduced to immigration hardball and a heartbreaking bargain. I was stunned but knew there was no choice in the matter. In a tearful meeting, I explained the situation to Miguel and Celia. Celia would have to return to her country. Ana would have to travel alone to the U.S. and endure her open heart surgery and recovery without her mother's care. Shortly thereafter, Celia returned home and presented herself at the embassy. Ana's visa was granted, we made her flight arrangements and she was soon in the U.S. preparing for surgery.

Over my 20 years working as a humanitarian, I have experienced many unforgettable episodes of compassion, sacrifice and love. They all affect me deeply. What happened next was one of the most amazing of these episodes. Celia's immense love and devotion to her daughter would not be denied by borders, immigration law, danger or poverty. Without anyone's knowledge, she purchased an airline ticket to Havana, Cuba and then flew from Cuba to Mexico. With nothing in her possession but her courage and a prayer card in her back pocket, she found her way to the border in New Laredo, Mexico, walked across a bridge into Laredo, Texas and successfully reentered the U.S. Amazingly, she phoned some relatives who helped her to fly to New York. She boarded a bus and to my utter amazement walked into my family room that night with her husband. It was a profound and stunning act of selflessness, courage, and motherly love and I marvel at it to this day. I'm glad to say that Ana's surgery was a success, that she is now a beautiful teenager and that her family is happy, successful and well.

The human side of this story is indeed remarkable but for our purposes here, my point is that at the very heart of this entire experience are the hope, opportunity and clinical capability that America presented to a desperate family. Our American system provided not just the opportunity for them to be productive and provide care for their loved ones but the platform, talent and capability to provide free surgical care to save the life of their child. It is the unique marriage of our collective wealth, represented by a proud children's hospital that had the will, technology and means to treat her disease, and the beautiful humanitarian soul of the cardiologist who agreed to help a child in need. It is this marriage, this unique combination of prosperity and compassion that we stand to lose; that we must defend and protect. It is only with a capitalistic, wealth generating machine that charity is possible. In most of the world, charity does not exist. We are a charitable people and it is a proud tradition. Prosperity is power; the power to effect change; to help those who suffer and bring hope to the hopeless. Seeking prosperity and the power it brings is neither moral nor immoral in itself. The moral question for each of us is how we decide to use that power. In a humanitarian sense, without prosperity, there is no charity. Without prosperity, none of the hope and miraculous healing in the above story would have happened. For me, this is the morality of wealth. The politics of envy are at work. The devolution into socialism and the fading of the paradigm of freedom are facts of life as you read this. Is this really what we want?

WHAT IS WALL STREET?

It is my observation that the majority of Americans, and especially our youth, has gained whatever they think they know about Wall Street from Hollywood. Recent movies like <u>Wall St.</u> and <u>Wolf of Wall Street</u> were extremely popular and entertaining and were seen by millions. For many people, those might be the only images they have of how our capital markets function. Unfortunately, in terms of providing any useful information as to the purpose and function of the enterprises we refer to as "Wall Street," they are completely useless. As a result, we are now gifted with ideas like the following gem from the New Left:

> *"Wall St. is greedy, reckless and they operate*
> *illegally. That's fine. But what do you do?"*

It's easy to be cynical and live in a world of caricatures without understanding the true nature of what surrounds you. Wall St. is a vast, extremely complex, global industry with the power to generate almost limitless capital, create tremendous wealth and finance remarkable human endeavor and enterprise; and to sometimes embarrass itself with gross excess and stunning human irresponsibility. But how sad would it be if the only image you had of our magnificent oceans was the trash that sometimes washes up on the shore. Go diving some time. You might see a whale and be awed by its size and beauty. It's true you might notice some ugliness: The pilot fish hanging off of it, the barnacles that grow on it and the parasites that feed off of it. You can choose to focus on that if you want to. But in so doing you will miss the bigger picture; the young calf by its side, the grace of its movements, the beauty of nature. You are badly mistaken if you think that *Wolf of Wall Street* or glib comments like those above have anything meaningful to say about the fundamental and positive role of capital and investment banking in our world.

On January 3, 2015, my company had the honor of ringing the closing bell at the New York Stock Exchange on the first trading day of the year. We were warmly welcomed in their vast and handsome conference room by officials from the NYSE. Prominently and proudly displayed in this room was a very large and beautiful Chinese vase. It was a gift from the Chinese to commemorate the largest initial public offering in world history. The offering was completed in 2014 and raised capital of $25 billion. The company was Alibaba, a Chinese trading and banking conglomerate that is revolutionizing business to business trade and banking in Asia and throughout the world. The success of that offering was, for a great many people, a complex and extraordinary accomplishment that will create immeasurable global commerce, jobs and wealth for people at all levels and walks of life. I guarantee you will never see a movie about it. It's not nearly as entertaining as a movie about a sleazy, everyday crook but its importance is far more profound and lasting. Such is the purpose and reality of Wall Street. Reckless and illegal? More like extraordinary.

As an aside, as I looked at the vase, I puzzled that this historic financial event could have sprung from China, a communist dictatorship that in its own way has discovered the power of capitalism to lift its people out of poverty. One might call their system Communistic Capitalism. It made me wonder how long free enterprise can survive in a communist dictatorship like China where the people are not free. Not long I suspect, but I digress.

The next time you open your MacBook or power up your Galaxy, or lace up your Nikes for a run ask yourself, "Where did the money come from to develop the product, build the plant, acquire the machinery and buy the raw materials to make them?" The answer is that it comes from our investment banking system; a complex, diverse, global system we simply call Wall Street. While incredibly vast and complex, it serves a very simple purpose. It is the conduit through which people and companies raise the capital they need to develop their ideas, dreams and products. It is the bone marrow and heart that create and pump the blood that fuels our collective economic body. Like our friend the whale, it attracts a lot of attention and there are always plenty of "parasites" who feed off the sheer mass of its being. Focus on them if you want, but you will miss the real story and its importance in our lives and the world.

To travel in certain political circles today, one must profess to be "against Wall Street." I scratch my head at this and wonder what they mean. Are these people against having plentiful, ready capital available to fund business development, jobs and growth? Do they object to their country hosting the world's most powerful source of funding for global growth and development? Are they against having a healthy flow of capital, (our country's blood flow) coursing through our country's economic body? Are they saying that they would prefer to have no such access to capital; to have no blood flowing in our system? If that's the case, then the countries I travel to would suit them perfectly; for they have none. Just for one day, try living in a world where there is no capital; where there is no blood in the system; where the talents, passions and dreams of millions of people are completely and utterly wasted.

DORA LORENA CEPEDA

I met Dora when she was four years old. Like Sonia Chavez, her story, on many levels, says a great deal about life in a broken country. Christmas is not necessarily a happy time for children living in poverty. Throughout Latin America, children go out on Christmas Eve and beg for candy in the streets. Their hope is that people in passing cars will throw them something. It is very dangerous but there are no authorities to control it. On Christmas Eve, 2005, Dora went out to a nearby highway near Pallatanga with her older brothers and sisters. Her sister, Sarah Noemi, held her hand but when her older brother darted across the highway, Dora let go, ran after him and was immediately hit by a car. It was rainy and very cold that night and Dora, badly injured and bleeding profusely, was carried to a nearby shack for shelter. She remembers the rain. Her mother arrived shortly thereafter and found Dora in shock and unconscious. Neighbors said that she would probably die. Dora's mother was determined to seek help for her but because of the amount of bleeding no bus or taxi would agree to take Dora to the hospital that, by the way, was two hours away. In addition, the family had no money. Finally, a neighbor offered some money and a taxi driver agreed to take Dora to the Children's Hospital in Riobamba. On arrival, Dora was taken into the hospital but, being Christmas Eve, there was no one there to treat her. To the best of my knowledge, Dora received no care or pain medication for at least 12 hours after her horrific accident. The next day, she was seen by a doctor who repaired her broken hip but was unable to treat her badly injured and broken lower leg and ankle. She received no further care for almost three months until the day we met. And on this day, her mother saved Dora's life for the second time.

I had organized a surgical team in the U.S. that would travel to Riobamba in March, 2006. It would be my second surgical trip to the city that is now my second home. I had never had an orthopedic component on a trip before but this team, oddly enough, had three orthopedic surgeons. I will never forget them. Somehow, Dora's mother heard we were coming and on our screening day at the local hospital, she presented Dora to us. Her leg had become infected after her accident and the infection had progressed untreated for nearly three months. The infection was now osteomyelitis and it had progressed far up her injured left leg. The last advice Dora's family had received was to amputate her leg. I believe Dora would not have survived this. Our talented surgeons were not able to repair Dora's extensive injuries but they did save her leg. Before and after her surgery, I spent a great deal of time with Dora and developed a strong affection and love for her. I promised her and her family that I would do whatever I could to find surgical care for her in the U.S. With great sadness, I left her in Riobamba at a facility that could care for her in a way her family could not due to their extreme poverty. Upon returning to the U.S., I began to seek help from the Shriners Hospital in Springfield, Massachusetts who, after nearly a year of waiting and hope, agreed to accept her for care.

When Dora finally arrived in the U.S. for her care, she lived with us at home for several months. Something happened one evening that brought home a sad aspect of life in poverty that I had not fully realized. Dora seldom complained and it was rare for her to cry. We had to give Dora a chlorine bath every evening. Given the method of treatment, the use of an external fixator and the condition of her leg, we had to be super vigilant about infection at all times. After her bath, we put her to bed upstairs as we always did. Later, my wife and I heard her crying softly up in her room and I went up to see what was wrong. I found Dora crying and staring out the window as if she could see all the way to Ecuador. I asked her why she was crying and she began to tell me that she had two little baby brothers but that they had both died around the time they were born. This, she said, made her very sad. I comforted her as best I could and the next day spoke with Olga Zapata in Ecuador, who knew the family situation well. She confirmed that, unfortunately, it was true that Dora had lost two little brothers at birth. You see, it is quite common in Ecuador for families to have 10-12 children and there are usually one or two that don't survive. Babies are often born in the home with midwives in conditions that are dirty and dangerous. Mothers have no voice or control in family planning and suffer raising so many children in gross poverty. In our caravanas, my staff has tried to raise the subject of family planning, tubal ligations and vasectomies but the husbands will not allow it and they prevent their wives from seeking help.

Child psychology experts identify several major forms of child trauma. They include: a serious accident, major surgery, abandonment, abuse and the loss of a sibling. My dear Dora was unfortunate enough to endure them all. Her great strength in surviving and overcoming these experiences is perhaps why I love her so much. That she is now safe and part of our organization is a true blessing.

Let me say here that Dora's story developed over many years and I can't retell it here in its entirety. Suffice it to say that one year later, Dora arrived in the U.S. with a badly deformed leg ready for what would be a year of difficult and painful surgery and recovery. With outstanding and complex care at Shriners, her leg was repaired and was soon stronger than mine. A few words about the method of care might be of interest. Dora's leg was repaired using what is called an External Fixator, or, an Ilizarov. The technique was pioneered by Gavril Ilizarov, born to a poor Jewish family in

Poland in 1921. After studying medicine, Ilizarov was sent to work in a hospital in Siberia. Many factories were moved to Siberia away from the Russian front. He began to develop theories about bone growth and the effect of tension in bone restoration and repair. He experimented with parts from a local bicycle factory and developed systems to repair bones from outside the body using complex rings, rods, posts and screws to adjust tension along multiple planes. His work was very successful and, unbeknownst to him, his techniques became famous throughout the world. In 1968, he was summoned by the Russian government to treat 1964 Olympic Champion high jumper, Valeriy Brumel, who was injured in a motorcycle accident and underwent many surgeries without success. It is said that it was only then that Ilizarov knew the extent of his world-wide fame. Shriner's surgeon, Dr. John DeWeese, used computer projections to estimate the ultimate size of Dora's bones and stature and designed a fixator and plan to, at the same time, lengthen, rotate and straighten Dora's badly broken leg. An interesting side note: the computer projections ultimately proved to be inaccurate in terms of Dora's growth resulting in some late corrections. I am convinced that the computer had no way of factoring in the extent of Dora's malnutrition when she arrived in the U.S. Once Dora discovered food and began to grow as she should, the computer model was history.

A team of three loving families here in the U.S. took turns caring for Dora. She returned to the U.S. twice, and learned, forgot and relearned both English and Spanish during her ordeal. Living now with her family back in Ecuador, she and her sisters have endured more trauma due to her family's dire poverty. Dora is now 15 years old and she is still like a daughter to me. Her family lives in an apartment around the corner from the clinic and she and her sister Noemi attend a private school thanks to a local friend of Fibuspam. I have great hope for them but fear for them every day. Both she and her sister spend their afternoons helping at the clinic in a safe and loving environment. They wear their Fibuspam vests with pride and I love to see them working as volunteers. For them, and for many others, the clinic is like a family and is a refuge from the many dangers that surround them.

THE CHALLENGE OF FREEDOM

We can see now how free enterprise derives its legitimacy and power by respecting man's free will and providing a natural mechanism for its economic expression. It is, in fact, the only mechanism of its kind. It draws its immense power and potential from the human spirit it serves. But this power by itself does not guarantee morality and in that, capitalism or free enterprise is neither moral nor immoral. It is simply the best means to organize the economic lives of free men and women. The challenge to each and every one of us is not simply to participate fully in the economic life that surrounds us but to use it for ends that are noble, fair, and honest. There are two very positive things that we should teach our young people. First, that there is a seat at the table for all people who wish to participate. More importantly, we need to teach our young people not just how the system of free enterprise functions and how to enter it but how to use it responsibly, with honesty and integrity in a way that is morally sound. Our young people have seen more than enough movie stereotypes of greedy businessmen and read enough about scandals to know the excesses that our system can produce.

But when do they ever hear about the millions of businesses and owners that strive every day to find a balance between shareholder return and corporate responsibility both to their employees and to their communities? They are all around us every day creating the jobs and wealth on which our society depends. It is time we began appreciating and teaching the fundamentals of the unique and special system we have.

Our system has evolved a great deal in very positive ways. A century ago and during the industrial revolution the worlds of workers and owners were very different and their interests were usually at odds. This brought the rise of labor unions, and significant strife and sacrifice brought change and a dramatic evolution in the relationship between owners and workers. Today, the lines between owners and workers have blurred and blended creating a powerful and positive new paradigm that is exciting to participate in. There are few companies remaining that don't recognize and respect the common interests that both parties share in today's modern, global economy. Many workers, in fact, now own shares in the companies they work for. The majority of Americans today participate in our ownership society by virtue of mutual funds, IRA's, ESOP and 401k plans. It is a powerful formula, unique in the world and it offers great potential. From its height in the 1950's at over 35% of the American workforce, union membership now stands at less than 7% in the private sector. While there are certainly those who would disagree, this new relationship is a glowing testament to the strength and evolutionary nature of free enterprise. It is something we should be proud of as a nation and it is a model for many others. Are we quite so sure we are ready to give this up?

People imagine socialism as a utopia of fairness and kindness where people care more for each other. I can tell you that the reality of socialism is something very different and much more serious and its results are quite the opposite. The desire to care more for each other is best accomplished in a democratic capitalist paradigm; where we value individuality, ambition, and success; where we use our freedoms to build wealth, individually and collectively in a moral, responsible and sustainable fashion; and where we share the fruits of our labor with others. This is our highest and best use as Americans and human beings. A deliberate, national commitment to both the common good and to the shared prosperity that makes it possible is one our country and every citizen could rightly be proud. Instead of abandoning our capitalist traditions, it is high time for us to renew our commitment to such freedoms. There are scores of countries adopting free, but fragile, markets that look to the U.S. for guidance and leadership; that expect us to be an example of a free people making sound economic and social decisions. And do not forget that the management of our finances here in the U.S., the strength of our dollar and our markets, and the soundness of our debts, hold immense importance in the economies of countless countries around the world. The lives of millions of people depend on us more than you know.

Paul R. Martel

Leading the world in economic freedom is a responsibility we appear to be abdicating. Should we regain our focus, there is an opportunity of immense potential to create positive change and unleash untold potential in a world desperate for a chance to succeed.

Capitalism On Trial

As I mentioned earlier, upon returning home from my trips I am always struck by attitudes, statements and opinions that run contrary to the traditions that have made our country so economically strong; that echo the socialist paradigms of the broken countries I've just returned from. Here, I would like to examine some examples of these and examine them more closely.

25% of all corporations pay no taxes.

I hear this often in different forms. As distortions and fabrications about our economy, corporations and business owners go, this one is the whopper. Allow me to point out the truth.

First, it must be understood that the large majority of businesses that make up our economy are small or medium size companies. Because it is more flexible and efficient than organizing as a C-Corporation, most of these millions of businesses organize and function as Subchapter S ("Sub S") corporations. This is as normal as having popcorn at the movie theater. As with my own company, it is true that Sub-S entities pay no taxes. This is because the business's income or profit flows directly through to their owners as income that they then report on their own tax returns. No one is avoiding anything, no one is using a special tax break, no one is benefiting. There is no unfairness and these people are not fat cats. They are your neighbors. The owners pay the taxes on the income from their businesses on their personal federal and state returns at their individual tax rates. For anyone to suggest that any of these people are taking advantage of anyone or benefitting unfairly is a gross lie. Leading progressive candidates know this as do all the other politicians who foist this drivel on the public. Shame on all of them.

Second, if we simply want to focus on large corporations, the statement is still grossly false. I chose at random from our own company's stock list 10 large, public corporations and looked at the taxes they pay. The data is as follows for each in 2014:

Company	Taxes Paid	Effective Tax Rate
Kohl's	$ 482,000,000	36.7%
CostCo	$1,100,000,000	33.9%
Cimarex	$ 298,000,000	37.1%
Am. Express	$1,900,000,000	34.5%
Amgen	$ 427,000,000	8.1%
Chicago Br.	$ 271,417,000	29.9%
Cisco Sys.	$1,860,000,000	19.4%
Monsanto	$1,000,000,000	28.2%
Ecolab	$ 476,000,000	28.4%
Mccormick	$ 146,000,000	26.3%

Every one of these companies paid hundreds of millions of dollars in taxes, and four of them over a billion, in 2014. The average tax rate for the 500 largest US corporations is 30%. The US has the highest corporate tax rate in the developed world and in addition, is the only major industrialized country that levies taxes on foreign profits. For politicians to paint our public companies as corporate thieves is a national disgrace. While I am hardly suggesting they are all as pure as the driven snow, they are vital to our way of life in many respects and we are foolish to disparage them so irresponsibly.

Third, companies are like people; at any given point in time there are healthy ones and not so healthy ones. In any given year, there will always be a significant percentage of companies that are not making money and therefore would not owe any tax. An example would be 2015 in the energy sector with the price of oil dropping from $110 per barrel to less than $30. Companies that explore for oil, refine it, transport it, etc. will have very significant losses this year. Thus, they will pay no tax. In any given year, there will always be thousands of companies who are struggling and losing money and, with no income, will pay no tax. Is this, too, part of this great unfairness fairy tale?

> *The middle class is shrinking. The rich are getting richer and the poor are getting poorer. Capitalism doesn't work and we need an activist government to create more income equality.*

It is true that census figures do show that the middle class has been shrinking for decades. We often read "The Middle Class is Losing Ground" in headlines and some politicians use the data to imply that the system is failing, that millions are falling into poverty and that we need more government activism and intervention. When you look at the census data, however, it paints a much more complex picture. Since 1971, the share of U.S. adults living in Middle Income *households* has indeed shrunk from 61% to 50%. But over the same period, the share of *households* living in the Upper Middle and High Income has risen from 14% to 23%. Over the period from 1967 to 2014, the percent of U.S. *households* earning $50,000 per year or less has shrunk from 58.2% to 46.8% while the percent of households earning $100,000 or more has grown more than three-fold from 8.1% to 24.7%. From the data we can conclude that people are indeed leaving the middle class but that they are rising to levels of greater income not the other way around. Which is it? Is America's middle class losing ground or rising into higher income levels? The answer is difficult to discern. Since 1967, the definition of *households* here in the U.S. has changed dramatically. Today, almost every U.S. household has two wage earners and these *households* do indeed have more total income. But it is also true that this total income is less and less able to support the growing costs of housing, health care and education. The real problem of the last several years seems to be stagnating or lower income levels in all categories due to a feeble economy and sharp increases in living expenses that hit hardest in the middle and lower income categories. The dramatic entry of women in the workplace, and the advent of the two-earner household explain much of the middle class statistics. The American worker is indeed struggling and we need more than demagoguery, sound bites and class envy arguments. The root problem is not capitalism itself but the dampening effects of immense debt, unprecedented growth of government, globalization and technology.

> *Capitalism is unfair and causes*
> *income inequality.*

As discussed previously, there are many who use the politics of envy and class warfare to gain power. Sadly, this is now evident in our domestic politics. Phrases such as "level the playing field," "fairness," "income inequality," "tax breaks for the rich," gaming the system," "loopholes," "different set of rules," and "fat cats" are misleading and have a singular purpose: To cause us to compare ourselves to others and to conclude that someone or some group has more than we do and, more importantly, that this someone or some group has more *because* we have less. You are meant to conclude that, because free enterprise is unfair, you have less, because someone has more. How unfair indeed! In this, we betray a fundamental and dangerous misunderstanding of how free enterprise works. Let's start at the beginning. How is wealth created? First, it is not created by government. Government collects taxes to provide services and redistributes wealth to achieve specific societal goals. Government does not create wealth nor does it create jobs. This is the job of the private sector. Wealth is created as follows: a man or woman has an idea for a product or a service they think there is a demand for. They go to the bank or to the capital markets where they borrow capital to finance their idea. The idea is a success, revenue is generated in excess of expenses creating profit, and the loan is repaid. Wealth has been created. A successful business is born, more dollars now flow through the bloodstream of the American economy, more taxes flow to the government and, in the process, more jobs are created. The main point is that the founder of this business took nothing from anyone. His success did not come at the expense of another. The person has created wealth that did not exist before. To think of our free enterprise system as a closed loop where one person's gain comes at the cost of another is to miss the entire point of our expanding system of enterprise. In socialist countries, there is little or no wealth creation; only redistribution. What little wealth there is, sloshes around via the government; spent and taxed, spent and taxed and finally exhausted. The pie never grows and the focus is always on who gets what piece. Given any set of circumstances, we should always opt for creating more pie rather than focusing on who gets what share. Today's leaders should encourage people to make more pie, not pit us against each other in fits of envy.

> *Big corporations pay outrageous*
> *executive compensation that is unfair to*
> *workers and to society. The government*
> *should pass laws to prevent it.*

I hear this complaint often and it is always delivered with passion. There are, however, a few problems with it. First, what a private or public corporation decides to pay its executives is no one else's business but its owners or shareholders. To suggest that any citizens or their government have the right to take money from other private citizens or their enterprises on some random idea of fairness is absurd, illegal and unconstitutional. Beyond that, though a person might be shocked at the level of an executive's compensation, that compensation costs that person nothing. It does not impact him in any way. It is part of the cost of running an enterprise, again, decided on by its owners or shareholders. If the compensation harms the company or impacts other employee compensation negatively, the company will suffer and fail. It does not at all follow that because a company offers generous executive compensation packages, its employees are worse off for it. The opposite is more likely to be true. Further, the bulk of large corporation executive compensation is in the form of stock shares that have no impact on employee compensation and no impact whatsoever on any other private citizen. If the executive performs well and the company grows, everyone is well served. Lastly, whether we are talking about LeBron James or Warren Buffett, their value is set in a free marketplace in light of their unique talents and ability to successfully create wealth not just for themselves but for all of us. The suggestion that government has a role in setting or limiting anyone's compensation is unthinkable in the paradigm of freedom.

Taxes Matter

The issue of corporate taxes is a contentious one today and many decry the current wave of "inversions" as unpatriotic and the worst example of corporate greed. An inversion is where a domestic U.S. company merges with a foreign entity to move its tax base to that foreign country and thus lower its tax burden. I would like to examine this a bit and see what we can learn as a people.

As you read this, millions of Americans are evaluating in which towns and states they will live in based on the relative taxes they are likely to pay during their lives and at their passing. Part of this decision is the value they feel they do or do not receive for their tax dollar. Cities and states amend their tax and economic policies accordingly and should strive to deliver the best services they can for the tax dollars paid. If a state maintains a high, uncompetitive rate of taxation and its residents consistently feel that they do not receive good value for their tax dollar, they move elsewhere. It happens every day in the paradigm of freedom and we do not deride

our friends and neighbors for making such rational economic decisions. Wouldn't we all agree that our state legislators
have a responsibility to consider the needs of its citizens and
evaluate their tax policies relative to other states? More to
the point, would we ever tolerate state laws making such decisions illegal and preventing the free movement of its people?
Of course not.

The rational economic decisions of corporations are no
different. If businesses feel that their state taxes are too high
and that the state is not managing its affairs properly, they
will leave the state in order to better utilize their resources
for their employees and shareholders. In my own state, a
very large multi-national corporation has been warning our
state government for years that its tax burden was too high,
that it was not happy with how its very significant tax dollars
were being spent and lastly that the legislature was hostile to
its business constituency. After many decades in our state,
they recently announced they were moving their operations
elsewhere. Is this also unpatriotic? Should the legislature
have passed legislation to force them to stay? The answer is
the same, of course not.

Let us take the argument one step further. Like the states
in our union, large multi-national corporations live and compete in a highly connected and competitive global marketplace. Our U.S. based companies compete with companies
in Canada, China, Germany, India, etc. In order to compete

for customers, capital and workers, they must manage their expenses. Like the retiring worker in Connecticut or the small business owner in Colorado, taxes are an important part of their budget and bottom line. The U.S. corporate tax rate, 35 percent, is the highest in the developed world. We are also unique in that we are the only industrialized country that utilizes a "worldwide" system rather than the "territorial" system used by developed countries including Canada and Great Britain. Under a worldwide system, American corporations are also forced to pay additional tax on any profits earned abroad. These taxes are paid at the time such income is repatriated thus making it disadvantageous to bring foreign profits back home to the US. Thus, there are trillions of dollars locked overseas rather than being available for investment here in the US. The Economist explains:

> *The incentive is simple. America taxes profits no matter where they are earned, at a rate of 39% — higher than in any other rich country. When a company becomes foreign through a merger, or "inverts", it no longer owes American tax on its foreign profit. It still owes American tax on its American profit."*

It is high time we stop blaming our large global corporations for fleeing a tax structure that makes it impossible for them to compete. Despite the populist rhetoric we hear daily, corporations are not unpatriotic thieves and their demonization has got to stop. They are being legally and publically punished for taking the steps they are forced to take to survive. Should this continue, we will find ourselves like the Venezuelans who can pat themselves on the back for having beaten the greedy fat cats while they stand jobless in endless food lines day after day with no prosperity or opportunity at all. Corporations are easy targets and attacking them makes for great headlines and political speeches. The truth, however, is a little different. It is in all of our best interest to support tax policy that makes U.S. companies more competitive. Rather than having an intelligent dialogue and looking honestly at our national tax policy, we unfairly attack our corporations as irresponsible thieves. Using simplistic, populist arguments to attack a broad group without acknowledging reality is seriously hurting our country and its ability to grow and prosper. Corporations are not our enemy but the engine of our car. It is no less patriotic to avoid irresponsible domestic tax policy than it is for a family to move to New Hampshire to avoid ill-advised estate tax policy. Should the owners of our corporations just do nothing and watch their business fail? Is that really what is best for us? You might be surprised to know that the Treasury Department has now actually issued laws to eliminate inversions and force corporations to comply with our uncompetitive tax policy. This is foolhardy and does nothing to make our country competitive in the world. Amazingly, this idea pretends that we do not live in a global economy; that our corporations do not have actual competition; that the prices of their products don't matter and that their bottom-line results are irrelevant. What fairy tale world do they think we live in? Perhaps, like Venezuela, Congress will soon outlaw inflation eliminating that pesky problem too. The scapegoating of corporations has gone too far. Portraying our large international corporations as unpatriotic fat cats and enemies rather than as important partners in our shared prosperity is hurting us as a country. It is time we accept, understand and teach their unique economic challenges and support them rather than treat them as enemies. Our corporate leaders are not unpatriotic but they are tired of being treated as adversaries.

Profits Matter

We have discussed at length the fundamental importance of a profit motive in a free market and the substantial benefits that are created for a society when people compete, work hard, dream and pursue their own self-interest. In the Paradigm of Freedom, profits matter for both individuals, small and large businesses. In terms of our corporations, it is fundamental for all Americans to understand and accept that to attract capital in our global markets, corporations need to show that they can be profitable. Investment capital, the blood in the system, flows through our capital markets seeking market returns. Without profit, corporations cannot attract investment capital and will ultimately fail. Maintaining profitability is an immense challenge and can prove very elusive. Our multi-national corporations function

in a fiercely competitive environment with a variety of significant challenges. They include: rapid changes in technology
(see Blackberry), changes in consumer tastes and trends (see
Chicos), unforeseen shocks in supply chains (see Chipotle),
dramatic currency swings and political upheaval to name a
few. It is time we as a people took a more balanced and ma-
ture view of the role of profit in our world markets. Simply
accepting and parroting broad and simplistic denunciations
of large corporations and their "obscene and excessive profits" denies the complex reality of our modern economy and
the important roles these companies play. The fact that profits in large multi-national corporations are very large does
not make them evil or obscene, just bigger. The now common argument that profits are obscene simply because they
are big in scale is shallow and meaningless. Bigness, by itself,
may be dramatic but it signifies nothing. The relative economics are the same for all size companies.

Character Matters

There is no question that in America today, Capitalism is
on trial. I have tried to show that this is a dangerous and
misguided conclusion resulting from many factors: A poor
understanding of the role of free markets in a free society, a
disturbing lack of consensus as to the importance of a healthy
economic engine, a widespread apathy toward the excessive
and alarming use of debt to finance state and federal government spending that we cannot afford. It must be pointed

out, however, that sometimes businesses and their owners do not live up to the ideals we seek in a free society. Corporate scandals, thievery, tax evasion and other lawlessness erode confidence in our business community and open the door to widespread criticism and caricatures of greed and irresponsibility. Our business leaders at local, state, and international levels serve a critical role in the economic health of our communities and should be held to high ethical standards. To abdicate this responsibility and tarnish this role does great harm to our country. Again, civic education addressing both the potential and opportunity in forming a business as well as the business ethics and corporate responsibility that go hand in hand is sorely lacking in our schools. It is worth reiterating, however, that these faults are due to our natures as human beings and not the system of capitalism itself.

If capitalism is on trial, it is partly because of a nearly complete lack of attention in any positive fashion in American news or media. It's true that we have a few cable business channels with wall to wall business minutia. But when was the last time a local or national newscast reported the success of a local or national company; the release of an important new product or the challenges of its development, the signing of an important new contract, the hiring of 10 or 100 more people, the overcoming of a serious setback. These things are all the result of human endeavor, creativity and perseverance. They happen all around us every day and are ignored. You are 1000 times more likely to hear news about

Howard Stern than you are about local or national business leaders and their successes and challenges. In so doing, we have set our priorities and they are not in proper order. As I have said, it is a shock to come from an environment where there is no economic opportunity to one where our vital corporate culture is nearly completely ignored.

Jobs Matter

Over the last several election cycles, an odd pattern has developed that betrays an unfortunate lack of understanding and a willingness to misinform. Whenever a business leader steps up to seek elected office, they are immediately attacked for "cutting jobs" sometime in their past. This is unfortunate because many of these people have the skills to lead our country in a more productive direction. Let's examine this a bit. First, it needs to be understood that the nature of any business is to expand and contract. Businesses breathe, grow and sometimes struggle with their health just like people do. There is not a business owner alive who has not both created jobs and cut jobs. Except in unusual circumstances, there is not a one who set out to cut jobs. Their nature is to create them. Yet, we seem to have created the paradigm that any business owner who has cut jobs is suspect and unqualified to serve. If a prerequisite to political office is that the person has never cut a job, then no owner will ever qualify. This is both unfortunate and cruel because the reality is that economies expand and contract, shocking world events happen, companies experience competition, products go in and out of favor, accidents happen, and key people pass away. Business owners have no choice but to react to such events and manage their businesses and payrolls accordingly. To publically characterize all job cuts as heartless acts of profit seeking greed is a gross oversimplification and an insult to the majority of business owners who struggle with such decisions every day. There are certainly exceptions, particularly in the field of corporate reorganizations (think of it as the emergency room for failing businesses and not pretty in either sense). The nature of capitalism is to create not destroy, to innovate not stagnate and to expand opportunity not contract. It is a strange paradigm that seeks to denigrate those who use free enterprise to create opportunity because, from time to time, they must deal with adversity.

REALITY
WHERE DO WE GO FROM HERE?

A t this point, it makes sense to leave the realm of theory and logic and look at the economic reality in the United States of America in early 2016. My purpose here is to simply identify the forces that are buffeting our country and offer my observations; my goal being to show that simply abandoning our system of free-enterprise is not the answer. Our problems are complex and many are self-made. None of them are caused by capitalism or free markets. Let's take a look:

America's Debt

Fundamental to any discussion of economic health is the issue of debt. We are a country with national debt of over $18 trillion dollars. We pretend to have a law that limits the amount of debt our country can and will support. It is called the Federal Debt Limit. While a great idea in theory, it has become meaningless. It provides no limit whatsoever and we are fooling ourselves if we think it does. The Federal Debt Limit has been raised 74 times since 1962 and from $6.1 trillion to $18.1 trillion since 1997. Most recently, it has been raised 7 times under President Obama and seven times previously under George Bush. The debt limit equaled 63% of our nations GDP or total output in 1997. It now exceeds 100% of our GDP. By comparison, Greece's debt is now 175% of GDP. In August, 2011, our U.S. debt was downgraded for the first time in history by Standard & Poors. This is a significant warning sign. Several of our states are near bankruptcy, Puerto Rico is in default and cannot pay its debts, and we are beginning to see municipalities, like Detroit, in default. This is not prosperity but gross, collective irresponsibility. Further, while total national debt grows steadily each year, national incomes are declining. This is a formula for disaster. To put a finer point on it, take the case of Japan whose debt is 230% of its GDP. Japan's debt is so large that a rise in interest rates of only 2% would increase their interest cost such that they would have no money left over to run their country. Their entire national budget would be used simply to pay the interest on their debt. Is this what we want for our country? Our debt hurts our economy. The interest cost is staggering and sucks the life out of it. Like Japan, it puts us at great risk if interest rates rise. It is a sign that the growth, power and influence of government are far out of balance. Most importantly, though, it is evidence that our spending is out of control.

The fault is ours as a people. We have elected politicians who are giving us what we want without regard to our economic health. There are leaders who sound the alarm but they are ignored and punished at the voting booth. How can Congress assert any authority to control debt without the support of the people? Our national prosperity is neither a liberal or conservative issue. It is vital to <u>every</u> American and we cannot be divided on its fundamental importance. Both parties need to make a commitment to shared prosperity and fiscal responsibility. They need to be central to the platforms of both parties. If neither major party will do so, then perhaps it is time for a third party. We know as families that we cannot spend our way into prosperity. If we are spending and borrowing too much, we put our families at tremendous risk. If we have debt problems, we know perfectly well that the solution is not three more credit cards. Why can't we apply the same discipline collectively to our country's finances and why do we demonize those who try to correct it?

Unrestrained State and Federal Spending

Our country's debt problems are the simple result of federal and state governments refusing to live within their means. When spending increases annually and incomes are declining, we have an obvious and serious problem. Suggestions that our problem is that the rich are not paying their "fair share" of taxes are just not credible when we know that the top-earning 1 percent of Americans paid nearly half of federal income taxes in 2014 and the bottom 80 percent of Americans paid 15 percent. Gross lies about corporate taxation are also not helpful. A people cannot spend itself into prosperity. It is time we all demanded more responsibility from government to spend wisely. As discussed earlier, over-spending is not the fault of capitalism or its free markets but of irresponsible people willingly duped into believing that there are no limits to what they can collectively afford.

The single most important impediment in the control of spending in our public sector spending may be the role of Collective Bargaining.

Until the 1960's, it was generally agreed that collective bargaining in the public sector was unwise and constitutionally prohibited. Even Franklin D. Roosevelt, an ardent supporter of collective bargaining in the private sector, was opposed to it saying, "All Government employees should realize that the process of collective bargaining, as usually understood, cannot be transplanted into the public service.... The very nature and purposes of government make it impossible for administrative officials to represent fully or to bind the employer in mutual discussions with government employee organizations." In 1962, John F. Kennedy, issued Executive Order 10988 reaffirming the right of federal workers to organize and codifying their right to bargain collectively. The game changed immediately and now public-sector unions are some of the nation's most powerful special interest groups. The reality of public sector unions has dramatically changed the face and fortunes of America.

It has created perverse incentives and distortions in all levels of government resulting in unsustainable financial arrangements that would be unheard of in the private sector. The Wall St. Journal rightly said, "Public sector unions may be the single biggest problem...for the U.S. economy and democratic government." There are many reasons why this is so. The most evident is the following: In the private sector, the interests of owners and workers are naturally in opposition. Negotiations, by their nature, are adversarial. Each party has a legitimate interest in the enterprise; one party in the profits generated and the other, in seeking fair pay for their labor to produce the profit. Each of their interests must be in balance. In the public sector, there are no owners and there is no profit. There is no adversarial party. There is simply the taxpayer who has no more or less to gain from the public service being performed. Management, in this case elected officials, who in theory should be acting on behalf of taxpayers, are often controlled and elected by the public employee unions themselves. This is particularly true in elections to state and local offices and school boards. Thus, the public sector unions control both sides of the negotiation and are, in effect, negotiating with themselves. This was best articulated by Victor Gotbaum, the leader of District Council 37 of AFSCME in New York City who bragged in 1975, "We have the ability, in a sense, to elect our own boss." Because public agencies are static, workers are easier to organize and tend to remain so almost permanently. Most public agencies are also legal monopolies and citizens have no right to seek competitors should cost and inefficiency spin out of control. Public sector unions are well financed through employee member dues through groups like AFSCME, NEA and SEIU and have grown to be some of the biggest political spenders in America with astounding results. Their success has created bloated state and local budgets, outrageous, unsustainable compensation and benefit arrangements for public sector workers and unfunded pension obligations in the trillions. It is a system rife with perversity that naturally seeks to perpetuate itself and its power. In 2010, in the publication National Affairs, Daniel DiSalvo, an assistant professor of political science at the City College of New York concluded: "Public sector unions thus distort the labor market, weaken public finances, and diminish the responsiveness of government and the quality of public services. Many of the concerns that initially led policymakers to oppose collective bargaining by government employees have, over the years, been vindicated." The key question for all of us is, who represents the interests of the taxpayers? The answer is almost no one and the results are painfully obvious.

Globalization

Over the last 30 years, our economy has been dramatically altered by Globalization; the recent expansion and integration of commerce beyond borders and time zones made possible by stunning advances in communication technology, transportation and logistics. Globalization is closely related to the spread of capitalism. In the late 1980's, a global phenomenon occurred which some economists called "The Triumph of Capitalism." Countries all over the world adopted free enterprise systems and democratic governments and endorsed private ownership rights and the rule of law. Capital markets expanded throughout the world providing the economic fuel for emerging economies. They began to prosper and over the last 30 years, millions upon millions of people began to rise from extreme poverty and achieved better standards of living. It is, in fact, what many of us might wish for in our world and it is taking place in front of our eyes. There is one thing, though, that we did not anticipate. These people are competing with us! For better or for worse, we live in a world economy where capital, jobs, products, talent and ideas compete in a fiercely competitive global marketplace. Like all things in life, it has its dichotomies. On the one hand, we are able to buy products cheaper and cheaper and use the money we save on other things. Through global trading platforms like Amazon, eBay and Alibaba we find savings we never imagined. But as we do our shopping, we must acknowledge that we ourselves are putting our own domestic companies at an extreme disadvantage. It is high time we stop blaming capitalism for the fact that we all shop for the lowest prices! It's true we don't want starving families in India but their emergence and success puts stress on our neighbors. It's not that free enterprise is not working, it's that it is working all too well! Let's examine a small example. For years, the U.S. has led in the manufacture of portable dental units, which make it possible to treat the poor in rural areas. A U.S. made unit typically costs about $4,500. China, which is becoming a fierce competitor in the dental field, now manufactures units that function well and cost less than $1,000. Because of globalization, the units are easy to buy and the savings are substantial. What is the U.S. manufacturer to do? Before we simply condemn the owner and our system as heartless we have to ask, "Exactly what choice does the owner have but to compete?" Do we expect him to just throw up his hands, fire all his employees and go out of business? Would you? I doubt not. The owner has no choice but to find a way to survive and protect his family, his legacy and as many employees as he can. And so he travels to China, hires local assembly workers, reduces his U.S. manufacturing staff and competes. Yes, he has to downsize and yes the U.S. loses more manufacturing jobs. But in the process, an interesting thing happens. The higher-level U.S. employees he keeps are highly educated and talented and they bring innovation to the company's products. The products are superior to the Chinese products and the company hires more and more higher-level engineers and designers as their sales increase around the world. This is the reality our country faces today. From a global, human perspective, this transformation is a wonderful thing. In many previously impoverished countries wealth and freedom are spreading and standards of living are rising. But domestically, it is creating a disheartening shortage of manufacturing jobs and a disjoint between the job skills of a large part of our population and the skills our economy is calling for. This is an education/job training problem and abandoning our capitalist system will not solve it.

Having said this, many Americans would be correct to say that globalization is a curse and is hurting them badly. It is true that foreign competition is complicated when the international playing field is manipulated by foreign government subsidies, our own minimum wage laws that may not always be helpful, unfair foreign labor practices, and irresponsible environmental policies. Here in America, we have accepted the higher cost that comes with clean air and rivers and basic protections for employees. Foreign companies that evade such cost make it impossible for our companies to compete. Those who consume foreign products are simply avoiding this cost. In this we are a schizophrenic people. We demand the lowest prices but wail at the damage we ourselves do to our own economy. Our national penchant to seek out the lowest price ignores the real societal costs that we have shouldered here in the U.S. to insure safety, protect the environment and provide fairly for our workers. This is a domestic policy problem and not the fault of capitalism. At the end of the day, our domestic companies have had no choice but to compete in the world as it is. Globalization is a powerful force in all our lives; but abandoning our free market system will solve nothing and throw the baby out with the bath water.

Technology

Technology has taken a severe toll on jobs and wages. Examples are all around us of jobs that have been eliminated by technology. Two examples will suffice. Mobile banking has nearly eliminated my trips to the bank and greatly reduced the need for tellers and processors. It saves me time but eliminates thousands of jobs. In another example, like many people, I recently refinanced a mortgage to take advantage of lower interest rates. I can remember 20-30 years ago, when a mortgage closing involved an entire room full of people. This one was completed electronically, entirely on-line without one meeting or human interaction. These two examples alone probably represent hundreds of thousands of lost jobs, most at lower income levels. Technology has brought significant rapid change and is having a major effect on our job markets. I think that part of the anger and frustration we feel as a people is that we are powerless to stop or keep up with the march of technology or its effects on our society. This is a challenge for us and will continue to cause stress in our system. But it is a gross untruth to say that capitalism and free enterprise are the cause of this economic stress. Indeed, there has never been a time when capitalism was more vital around the world. Those who blame free enterprise for the problems of globalization and technology are simply looking for an easy answer. Those who argue that the solution is more socialism are sorely mistaken. Save your anger and pity for the scores of socialist countries who are totally and hopelessly left behind; whose lost decades will soon become lost centuries.

Immigration

Our country's immigration system has been broken for decades. Without question, it affects our job markets and the cost of government, especially in border-states. Immigration's growing chaos is fueling anger and frustration and seriously damaging confidence in government. While our immigration problems have little or nothing to do with Capitalism, the source of the immense tide of immigration has everything to do with the lack of it.

Our current immigration firestorm began during the second Bush presidency with the bipartisan Comprehensive Immigration Reform Act of 2007 that sought to simultaneously strengthen our borders and address decades of immigration mismanagement by providing a path to citizenship for many illegal immigrants. The Act was never voted on. The country's political right would have none of it. They screamed, "Amnesty," rejected, and continue to reject, any solution to fix our past errors, and demand the deportation of millions of immigrant families. Their activism punished moderates at the polls and Republicans promptly lost the White House in 2008 and again in 2012. Strongly rejecting the right's obstinacy, many voters lurched to the left. Moderates on the left as well were punished, Hillary Clinton was dumped, Barack Obama was elected and a wide political chasm resulted. Through controversial executive orders, President Obama has liberalized our immigration laws, chosen not to enforce others, and created a confusing immigration patchwork that seems compassionate to some and unintelligible and irresponsible to others.

A Humanitarian's Defense of Capitalism

From my standpoint as a humanitarian, what is lost in all of this is any discussion of the fundamental cause of the immigration problem itself; the near collapse of society throughout Central and South America. Millions of people are taking unimaginable risks to escape two things: A gross and pervasive poverty that dooms people to lives of suffering and hopelessness, and an environment of violence more depraved than Americans can imagine or understand. On my first trip to Neiva, Colombia, near an infamous FARC stronghold called the "Despeje," I was given a tour of the hospital where we would work. A nurse took me to a third floor balcony overlooking a back parking lot. I looked down and saw that the parking lot was lined with dozens of body bags. Stunned, I looked up at the nurse who shook her head and simple said, "It's the violence." I knew at that moment that we Americans know nothing of the level of violence in these countries. I have a friend in Guatemala in San Juan Sacatepequez who is an accountant and loving father of three young girls. It is commonplace for him to receive phone calls at night from gangs who simply say, "We want 200 Quetzales or we will hurt your daughters." They aren't fooling. A few years ago, he was required to join a community group formed to confront the gangs. You see, there is no police or military protection for these people. None. Their countries are broken and bankrupt. There is nothing to protect them and they have had enough. And so, three nights a week, a man no different from you or me, donned a mask and, armed with a gun and a phone, terrified, walked the dark, dangerous streets of his town looking for depraved and heartless gang members. Coincidentally, at that time I happened upon a news item from their town about a gang member who was strung up and burned by the community to send a message to the gangs. I later asked my friend if he was there that night and he said, "No, but I heard about it." My Executive Director was nearly murdered by thugs who entrapped and jumped him with a gun and a machete on the streets of Guayaquil. The nephew of a good friend was brutally murdered in Riobamba by thieves who simply wanted his watch. In Colombia, it is common for children to be kidnapped for ransom. My foundation has treated children in the northern Ecuador city of Ibarra who are refugees seeking protection from the extortion, killing and gross violence in Colombia. This is life in most Central and South American countries. Is there no room in our national dialogue to at least acknowledge the gross poverty, suffering, desperation and violence that forces people to our borders? The majority of these immigrants are not criminals; they are people who can no longer tolerate life in this toxic and tragic soup of unending violence and poverty.

In my view, there are several causes of these conditions:

- The marriage of Marxist revolutionary groups with narco-terrorists.
- Widespread Cuban influence and their alliance with oil rich Venezuela.
- The exportation of kidnapping and extortion by Cuba to fund political action.

- The surprising neglect of the U.S. to the serious problems of our neighbors in our own hemisphere.
- A long history of massive corruption and mismanagement by any number of dictators and repressive, socialist governments.
- Centuries of repression, particularly among the indigenous populations, and the psychological scars of abuse, discrimination and gross poverty.
- Lack of education.
- A population of women who are powerless and often abused and who have an almost complete lack of reproductive rights.
- A persistent socialist paradigm.

Consistent with the message of this book, though, I reiterate that the problem in these countries is not the presence of capitalism or the free markets; it is the lack of them. There is simply no capital, no blood flowing through their systems. While many of these countries flirt with the idea of free markets, because their paradigm is not one of freedom, the ideas never really germinate and they quickly snap back into a socialist mind-set and are then further abused by populist dictators like Hugo Chavez or his many imitators. They are trapped.

I have tried to illustrate the real ramifications of the path we are on. They are not theoretical and they portend a society very different than the one we now know and enjoy. Like many others, I am ringing an alarm bell. Our country's economy limps along while state and federal governments spend more and more and pile up more and more debt. Government has become pervasive in our society and it is hard to identify any area of public life or economic activity where government does not now have a major role. This is not the America our founders intended.

What we must do is resolve to collectively and deliberately make sound local and national decisions to limit the growth of government and government spending and do what we can to repair and strengthen the engine of our economy. Those who articulate these values should not be ridiculed but supported. This must become an urgent national priority. We all have political and social issues that are important to us but we are all riding in the same car. We can argue about the air conditioning, or the CD player, or the need for a trailer hitch and a boat or power windows; but there comes a time when we have to care for the engine. Without it, nothing else works or matters. Now is that time. Later, when we are strong again as a nation, when the engine of our car is running well, we can consider adding more features to the car. For now, we cannot afford the spending and debt that we have and our engine is stalling from the weight. This is not sustainable.

We are well down the path of Democratic Socialism. Our apathy toward free enterprise is evident in election after election when it is always an afterthought. For some, abortion rights are a primary issue, for others, immigration, for others, the right to marry for gay couples. All are valid. But for all of us together as a people, there is only one primary issue on which everything else depends; the health and perpetuation of the economic framework from which we are fortunate to derive our livings, our collective wealth and strength. We can no longer pretend that it will take care of itself without our support.

A popular socialist with a microphone can easily point out the attractive benefits of a long menu of social programs and blame any number of boogeymen for our lack of them. That's the easy part. The trick is how to pay for them. Who wouldn't agree that free, high-quality education for all is a great idea? Who wouldn't support the goal of equal access to quality health care for all? But to pretend that a people can enjoy unlimited social benefits at no cost is a gross lie. Further, to advocate for such programs while at the same time condemning the economic engine we have to pay for them is just rank foolishness. Such people are leading us off a financial cliff in the pursuit of a fairy tale. There is nothing wrong with a people aspiring to a stronger, healthier, more educated society for all citizens; but the cost cannot be ignored any longer. It is long past the time for us to develop a shared future vision for our country. Such a vision must include a shared recognition of the fundamental importance of Capitalism, free markets, productivity and prosperity to pay for the things we value.

Our high schools and colleges must prepare our students to enter the economic world in which they will live, not teach them to oppose and discard it. Our youth should be inspired to succeed, as Richard John Nuehaus put it, to do well and to do good. Our youth must understand the relationship between freedom and capitalism and its fundamental role in our collective well-being. Do we think they will simply learn this passively through osmosis? Have we no responsibility to prepare them? They should be introduced to role models of entrepreneurs who conduct their businesses fairly and successfully and learn that these people are not their enemies. They should be cautioned not to be manipulated by envy but inspired to be the best they can be and to be respectful of the varied gifts and achievements of others. They should understand the reality of economic choices made by other countries and the real human costs of those choices. I believe these steps are critical at this time and I call on educators and local boards to address them before it is too late. In my view, it is tragic to send our students out into the world knowing little or nothing about our economic system and armed with nothing but cynicism.

The freedom to dream and to pursue your dreams is a blessing; not having it, a curse. Having access to the capital to make your dreams a reality is not vulgar; the lack of it is. In Capitalism, we have in life's toolbox the greatest tool the world has ever known to create prosperity. Be grateful for it. Pick up the tool and use it well; and then, go make a difference in the world.

THE SPIRIT FINDS A WAY

(From *"To The Least of These My Brothers"* by Paul Martel)

Humor is, however, nearer right than any emotion we have. Humor is the atmosphere in which grace most flourishes.

H<small>ENRY</small> W<small>ARD</small> B<small>EECHER</small>

To explain the nature of laughter... is to account for the condition of human life.

© 2006 Derek Dudek

D espite their difficulty and challenges, I should make it clear that surgical trips do have their lighter moments. Given the environment, sometimes the humor is a little dark and the source a bit strange. But we welcome a smile or a shared laugh like we would a sudden ray of warm sunshine in a bad storm. Sometimes it feels a bit surreal laughing uncontrollably in the midst of suffering but the brain and spirit have a way of finding a healthy balance and moving forward. A few examples will illustrate. The first took place in Neiva, Colombia located in the south bordering an area formerly known infamously as the Despeje. Colombians have been at war for over 40 years. Leftist rebel groups became co-opted by narco-terrorists in an intractable spiral of killing, kidnapping and torture. Colombians despair at the pain and suffering their beautiful country has endured. The Despeje is an area of land roughly the size of Switzerland which was ceded to the rebels in the late 1990's by former President Pastrana as a peace offering to encourage the main rebel group to enter peace talks. This was supposed to be a place where they could live in peace and structure their communities as they wished. There was tremendous hope that the violence might finally end but it was not to be and the gesture came to nothing.

The Despeje quickly became a haven for drug production and trafficking and a staging ground for terrorist attacks and kidnappings. An embarrassed and defeated President Pastrana was voted out of office and new, hardline President

Alvaro Uribe rescinded the grant of land in one of his first official acts as President. Thanks to the hard work and vision of the great humanitarian I supported, his teams have completed 11 medical trips to Neiva and have completed nearly 2000 surgeries there. Many of those children were children of FARC rebels. Neiva was a dangerous place and we were always heavily guarded when we were there. Two years earlier, a home near the end of the Neiva airport runway was filled with explosives set to blow as the new, visiting President's plane was due to land. The plot was discovered by police but while many of them were investigating, the house was detonated destroying many homes, killing many and injuring scores of children. So it goes in Colombia.

When we are there, the hospital is filled to overflowing with recovering children or others waiting their turn. The floors in the normally empty patient rooms are covered with thin mattresses to accommodate the hundreds of children and their families. It is always airless and hot on the 4th and 5th floors and the hallways and stairway landings are packed with beds, children and families. Other families stay at the local army base and are bussed to the hospital. Five days of surgery and the work that goes with it leaves us all exhausted in many ways. Near the end of a recent trip, one of our pediatricians had the severe misfortune of passing a kidney stone and was enduring his pain up on the fifth floor. Our lead surgeon had a minute to visit him and asked me to come along with him. As we weaved our way up through the crowds of families and recovering children, he began telling me a story of an unfortunate young boy who had had his cleft palate operated on so many times that he had been left with a loud whistle when he spoke. The surgeon began to affect a long imaginary conversation with the boy and each answer was a pathetic but hilarious whistle. And he went on and on jabbering and whistling as we weaved our way toward our suffering friend.

I think often about some of the cases we had seen on that trip. I remember little Maria, an orphan abused by her father, burned by her brother and abandoned by her mother, held in the loving arms of the nun who had taken her in and who brought her to us to ease the pain of her burns. A group of us had stood in tears by her bed as the nun recounted her story. I remember the young man, whose parents had both been killed in the violence, who later nearly died of a laryngospasm after his surgery. I remember the faces of two thirteen year old children who were kidnapped by depraved rebels near our hotel to extort money from their poor families. I remember the young, teenage boy with the badly burned chest, whose parents had both been killed by the FARC, all alone with no one to help him, trying to be so tough but finally crying when he understood the extent of the surgery he would need. And I remember walking with my friend through the heat, hunger, pain and crying, both of us laughing like whistling fools, taking in a light moment like desperate divers surfacing for a precious breath. Language is always a great source of humor. I remember a time with my great humanitarian friend, Zorayda, walking together through the hospital in Machala, Ecuador. She met a good friend along the way and they stopped to chat. I stood aside and waited while they talked in Spanish. When they parted, she sensed my exclusion and to draw me in she exclaimed in her own brand of English, "He has crabs!" Being near the coast I knew that she meant he had a crab farm but I quickly explained to her what any American would think she had said. We laughed a long time over that one. When asked, "How are you?" Zorayda would often say "Pura vida!" a Spanish response popular in Costa Rica meaning "Pure life!" One morning, I was surrounded by a group of nurses who asked in Spanish how I was doing. "Here's my chance," I thought, and, beginning to learn some Spanish myself, proceeded to answer loudly, "Puta vida!" unwittingly declaring that I was the whore of life. We all had a good laugh and it was a great way to start the day.

But the best illustration of the resilience of the human spirit comes from my experience with a nurse named Sheila who brought it to life for me. Sheila was the recovery room nurse I worked with in Cartagena, Colombia on my very first trip. She was a veteran nurse who had suffered from breast cancer and was at that time recovering from recent, radical surgery. Yet, here she was, giving of herself gleefully in the slums of Cartagena helping poor children. Sheila had reason to give up; reason to be angry and depressed didn't she? Instead, her attitude was always generous, encouraging and helpful. She joked that her figure was brand new to her and laughed often and openly about her condition. She had an infectious laugh and was always alert to a humorous or heart-warming moment in recovery. She worked long hours like everyone and never complained. She spoke not one word of Spanish but by the time we left, she was the friend of every local nurse she worked with. During the trip, we encountered a rare case of a young teenage girl who had a single toe that would not stop growing. Luckily for most of us, our genetic code tells our fingers and toes how long they should be and when to stop growing. This girl had one toe that wasn't getting the message and she would have suffered with this deformity for the rest of her life. She had trouble walking and couldn't wear shoes. I imagined she would probably never dance, have a boy-friend, marry or have children. Our senior surgeon decided to do an amputation that would take care of her problem and as a result, she would be able to live a normal life. The surgery was successful and, it being a rare case, the hospital insisted that the immense toe be sent to pathology for study. It was placed in a big jar filled with clear fluid and, to Sheila's deep, deep dismay, ended up on top of the medicine cabinet in our busy recovery room. And there it stayed all week long, a constant source of irritation to Sheila, and a wellspring of potential humor.

Midway through that same trip we had a child who came out of the OR after 8:00 at night who did not do well in recovery. I don't remember why; perhaps bleeding or problems breathing after anesthesia. It happens. A few of us decided we needed to stay to either care for the child or just lend support. By midnight, our small group had been working for nearly 17 hours straight. We had not eaten, we were very tired, and we needed to get some sleep to prepare for the next early wake up call. When it was finally alright to leave, we found that the main hospital entrance was locked up and we had to find our way out through other wards and dark hallways. There is nothing more quiet and peaceful than a hospital at 1:00 AM. Families were asleep together on cardboard in the hallways and in the courtyards. The sick and injured lined the dark hallways staring up at us as we trudged by in our scrubs.

©2006 Derek Dudek

Suddenly, a young local resident we did not know ran up to us and begged us to help him with an emergency case he could not handle. He told us a teenager had fallen off his bike, was then hit by a car and suffered severe trauma to his head. Despite his bleeding and injuries, we were told that he had been turned away from three other hospitals because he could not pay and finally ended up at Hospital del Ninos. The resident was worried that the child would die and he had neither the drugs nor skill to help him. "Please, help me!" he pleaded. We all looked over at our own exhausted surgeon who did not know what to say. We talked and he concluded that this was not our patient; that we were not there to support their emergency room; that our own supplies of drugs and narcotics were getting low and that if he did not get some sleep, he would not be able to treat his own patients. Further, as a doctor, once he began treating the patient, he had a moral obligation to continue the treatment, something he could not do. We knew he was right on every count and we all hated it. We said no to the sweating young resident and, God help us, we walked away from him. We walked out into the night to our cab, out into the dirty street with the mangy, roaming dogs, through the old, broken gate, past the useless guard and the many, tired poor people still gathered around the hospital.

The surgeon took the front seat of the beat-up cab and I slumped into the back with Maria, a former nun and worldly scrub nurse with wide humanitarian experience. In the quiet of the cab as we waited for the driver, Maria began to cry. We sat there together in the darkness of the Colombian night while she sobbed. She cried for the people of the barrio. She cried over the massive poverty, the desperation, suffering, hopelessness, and illness. She cried for the scared young doctor who couldn't help his patient. And she cried for the bleeding boy who had been turned away from three hospitals because he had no money.

Yes, Sheila really hated that toe. She told me that constantly and she made the funniest face every time she saw it. But there it was, every day on the cabinet in the jar waiting forever to be brought to Pathology. She'd look at it and make a funny, disgusted noise and we'd both laugh. It became a very funny private joke to us. When dignitaries came to visit we would stand them right next to the cabinet to talk and, clueless to it all, their heads would be right next to the toe. Golly, that was funny. Whenever we were interviewed or photographed by the press we always stood by the toe so it would be in the picture with us like it was our pal. During the long days, we'd glance at the toe and laugh inside and some of the local nurses began to notice our little joke and laugh with us. Yes, Sheila really hated that toe and I always smile to think about it and about her. And I like to think the girl who had it is dancing somewhere in Colombia.

In the cab, Maria's crying slowly subsided. She spoke to the doctor calmly but firmly insisting that he go back and help the young resident and his patient. He relented and trudged back to the hospital. As it turned out, the situation was not as grave as we feared, he gave the resident and patient the help they needed and returned to the cab about an hour later. We drove off to the hotel in silence to catch a couple of hours sleep and prepare for the next day.

©2006 Derek Dudek

Conclusion

In this book, I have tried to demonstrate that capitalism is the economic expression of the freedom on which our country is built; that having capital to finance our dreams and innovation is a blessing, not a curse. Capital and the complex institutions that create and provide it are the heart and blood of our collective economic body. To say that one is against these things is foolhardy to the extreme. I have argued that the Paradigm of Freedom is the most moral environment for human beings to realize their unique potential, seek meaning and purpose in their lives, enjoy the fruits of their own labor, pursue their own dreams and happiness, and realize their own ability to provide for themselves and their families and share with others. As Americans, we do not accept that the individual is simply a faceless cog in a tyrannical mechanism that seeks to impose collective equality. I've expressed dismay at the growing percentage of Americans that welcomes the idea of socialism. This is despite the absence of any proof or example whatsoever that the socialist model has ever served a people well except to provide more poverty, hopelessness and financial failure. Pointing incorrectly to the Nordic Model as a socialist success story is a gross falsehood. The history of socialist failure is long and painful and there is more than ample evidence in our time around the world.

The proof is all around us, currently and historically, that the pursuit of income equality is a fool's errand. I have tried to show that globalization and technology, not capitalism, have taken an immense toll on manufacturing employment in the US. We live in a unique time in a growing, more connected and competitive world and these are problems we can overcome. Blaming capitalism for the loss of manufacturing jobs and lack of income growth at the lower income levels is an absurdity and a corruption of our country's strongest and most fundamental freedoms. The modern progressive movement is peddling a utopia that has proven to fail over and over again with disastrous, deadly and irreversible results. Those who chose to follow this path are dooming us to the same result. A country already shouldering debt far beyond its means to pay can hardly afford to borrow more to pay for more social benefits, regardless of how worthy they are. Without a well running, healthy economic engine creating jobs and prosperity, we have no money to pay for anything and we will continue to lose our freedoms and the quality of life we have had the privilege of enjoying for so long. The business owner, the business community and our system of capital creation are not the enemy but the well from which we draw our collective prosperity and economic strength. The denigration of capitalism, its participants and its entities is a disgrace to our country and an abdication of a responsibility we owe to a world that looks to us for leadership.

I owe my life as a humanitarian to my success as a capitalist; to the prosperity my company has been able to produce over its nearly 30 years. Without that prosperity, I have nothing to share with others. In identical fashion, the prosperity generated by our country's free enterprise, capitalist system is the engine that supports the social contract we seek as a people. Without prosperity, my clinic cannot change lives every day. Without our collective prosperity, there is no social contract. Unsupportable debt and spending is not prosperity; it is a charade that will inevitably collapse under its own weight.

Throughout my sixteen years of humanitarian work in dramatically broken countries, the reality of life in a socialist paradigm has not been theoretical to me. I have seen its effects up close and witnessed its hopelessness, poverty and suffering. As you read this, countries around the world are collapsing from the weight of the tyranny and nonsense of socialist economic policy. Is this what we want for our country? There is no evidence whatsoever that our experience with socialism would be any different than the countless other countries it has ravaged. Yet, we seem blind to that

Paul R. Martel

certainty and blind to the extreme dangers we already face as a result of our apathy. I do not want to lose the profound blessings I am so proud to rediscover when I reenter the US after my trips; blessings we as a people are taking for granted. I am hopeful that our citizens will think twice before discarding a system that is the model for much of the world; that they will reject the shallow arguments of those who propose empty, over-simplified solutions to complex problems, who manipulate voters with envy instead of providing truth and intelligent solutions. Lastly, I am hopeful that our youth will not so quickly and disdainfully abandon a tradition of prosperity that they know little about but which has served their country, and them, extremely well; a tradition of economic freedom that has provided them a society rich in the quality of its services, institutions and benefits and unlimited in the breadth of its freedom and opportunity.

nformation can be obtained at www.ICGtesting.com
the USA
1944290616

RV00001B/12/P